Home Storage

By Richard V. Nunn

Library of Congress Catalog Card Number: 75-12122

Manufactured in the United States of America

First Printing 1975

HOME STORAGE

Editor: Grace Hodges
Cover Photograph: Taylor Lewis
Schematic Drawings: Ralph Mark

Contents

Introduction

You may think you have all the built-in storage you have room for and that a 100 by 200 square foot, tin-roofed warehouse in the backyard is the only answer to your storage problems. *Home Storage* is designed to show you how to make more efficient use of the space in your home or apartment and to help you do it economically.

The book is divided into two sections. The first section, Chapters I and II, is devoted entirely to storage ideas: finding storage in existing space and using it. The second section, Chapters III, IV, and V, shows how to build storage into your home yourself. We mention only the basics in the second section. There are no gimmicks or hard-to-do construction techniques involved. In fact, if a special piece of equipment will be needed to build a fancy cabinet door, we say so, but we give you an alternative, too, which may be easier and fit your handyman skills better.

By utilizing both sections and adding a pinch of your own imagination, we think you will be rewarded with a smoother running household, free from the daily "mess" that inadequate storage — or unplanned storage—produces.

Carefully Planned Storage

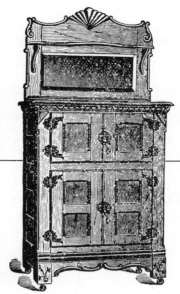

Storage space, generally, does not rob you of valuable floor space. Carefully planned, it can add to the dollar value of your home and actually *increase* the livability in and around your home.

Define your storage problem

Ask yourself these questions:

• Do I already have storage space? If so, is this space *inadequate* or simply *unorganized?*

• If I build a new storage unit, what exactly do I want the unit to do? Could this additional space and investment be better organized to do several jobs instead of just the one job I have in mind?

In many residences, storage space sometimes is adequate but *unorganized.* For example, a drawer where silverware is kept may be as mixed up as a jigsaw puzzle in a bushel basket; a 79¢ silverware tray may be the answer. Or perhaps the kids leave their coats and boots scattered on the living room floor; is closet space lacking, or is the closet space unorganized?

On the other hand, the need for *additional* storage may be the result of the accumulation of personal and household belongings such as clothing, books, toys, kitchenware, tools, and equipment.

Look for more storage

Unlike gold, a spot for existing storage and new storage is not too difficult to find. In fact, existing storage space usually is obvious, and, of course, the obvious usually is overlooked. Here's a checklist of possible storage spaces:

• Under low windows on or under a window bench or seat

• On the ceiling over a bathtub
• On the wall over a lavatory
• Under open stairsteps in a basement
• Over an open hallway
• Between studs in a wall
• Next to a fireplace
• Across an open wall in any room
• Behind attic knee walls
• Between floor joists in the basement
• Between floor joists in the attic
• In room dividers
• In indoor/outdoor crawl spaces
• At the sides and end of a garage
• At the side or end of a carport
• Under a porch
• Under a deck
• In a soffit
• Over a suspended ceiling
• Under a corner table
• Under a roof overhang
• Under beds

Look for ideas

On the following pages you will find a large collection of storage ideas. The collection is *not* organized according to specific location of storage in a house or apartment; we want you to look for *ideas* that you can adapt to solve your specific storage problems. For example, one of our illustrations for kitchen storage may be more applicable to another room in your home.

STORAGE WALLS WITH PLENTY OF PIZZAZZ

There are two types of storage: built-in storage, such as storage walls, and freestanding storage, such as cabinets. The basic difference between the two is that a storage wall usually is a built-in, tailor-made unit, and a freestanding storage unit is a prefabricated cabinet that you simply set in place. Example: a wall closet as opposed to a kitchen cabinet.

The difference, really, is not too critical, but it might be helpful to distinguish between the two when you are designing storage and ordering materials for the project.

Built-in projects require materials such as 4- x 8-foot sheets of hardboard, plywood, hardwood-plywood, and particle board. Freestanding projects usually call for prefabricated cabinets, unfinished furniture, ready-to-finish drawer units.

Perforated hardboard, which is available in 4- by 8-foot panels and in ⅛- and ¼-inch thicknesses, is an excellent storage material. After being cut to the size you want, these hardboard sheets are mounted over furring strips. The furring strips project the sheets away from the wall surface so special hardboard hooks can be inserted into the holes. A wide variety of hooks are available to support pots and pans, utensils, decorative items, tools, shelving—almost any type of object you want to hang up and out of the way. The hardboard panels are brown in color; they may be finished with regular enamels, latex, or epoxy paint. Perforated hardboard may be used for storage anywhere in your home: the kitchen (as shown here), bathroom, living room, garage, or workshop.

Shelving is a storage standard. You can buy almost any type shelving you need at home center stores and building material outlets. Shelving units include wall standards and brackets as well as shelves. Shelves come prefinished in a variety of woods—oak, mahogany, or walnut. You may buy matching brackets or metal brackets to support the shelving, and you can add your own personal touches to the unit. Since the brackets usually are adjustable, you can position the shelves to suit your needs.

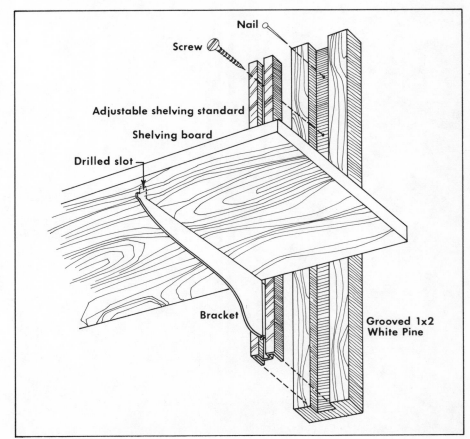

Nail

Screw

Adjustable shelving standard

Shelving board

Drilled slot

Bracket

Grooved 1x2 White Pine

A custom touch was added to this shelving unit by inserting the adjustable shelving standard into lengths of 1- by 2-inch white pine boards. To cut the grooves (or dadoes), you need a power saw with dado blades. If you don't have a power saw, use narrow strips of white pine material, and after the standards have been attached to the wall with glue, screws, and/or nails, butt the wood against the sides of the standards. Any other type wood can be substituted for the pine: oak, walnut, mahogany, maple, or redwood.

Custom-built shelving and storage cabinets fit into a niche between the fireplace wall and paneled wall. The same unit can be easily constructed by assembling several kitchen base cabinets and mounting them to the wall. The shelving can be installed with simple brackets over the base cabinets, which can have slanted tops of hardwood 2 by 6s mounted over angled framing members fastened to the cabinet tops. Unless you have power tool equipment, the base cabinets will be difficult to construct. We suggest that you stick to prefabricated and prefinished base cabinets or have a local millwork shop fabricate the units for you.

Far left:
This television/stereo center is easy to build into an existing closet storage area. The center is nothing more than several shelves held by adjustable shelf standards and brackets. The dividers for the records are ¼-inch tempered hardboard set in grooves (dadoes) cut in the shelves. If you don't have a power saw, you can form the grooves by attaching moldings to the shelving material. (See moldings in Index.)

Left:
Behind closet doors is an ideal spot for a stereo center. A vertical piece of plywood is used for one side of the unit; the walls form the other side and the back. By using adjustable brackets, you may arrange the shelves to fit the sizes of the records, tapes, and equipment.

The rustic look in this storage wall was accomplished with rough-sawn timbers for vertical shelving and table supports. The top shelves for books may be supported by adjustable shelf brackets; the bottom shelves are edged with 1- by 4-inch rough-sawn lumber to match the vertical supports. The countertop is notched to accept the vertical supports, and the wainscotting below is simply nailed to 2- by 4-foot cross members. The wainscotting can be replaced by small matching cabinets for additional storage.

This handsome storage wall consists of a series of raised panel doors hinged to vertical framing members. The unit has a false bottom, and the vertical members provide an off-the-floor design, giving the wall a floating look. The same wall can be created with louvered doors or standard bifold doors finished to match the room decor.

Barn siding, actually salvaged from an old barn, is used for doors on this storage center. The unit was conventionally framed. (See framing in Index.) Permanently fixed or adjustable shelves may be used. If real barn boards are scarce in your area, you can buy standard barn board paneling as a realistic substitute. The paneling comes in 4- by 8-foot sheets.

Regular barn door framing is used to carry out the rustic theme of the storage wall. The framing is nailed to the barn siding boards in a "Z" configuration. The trick here is to nail the top and bottom framing members to the siding first, then fasten on the vertical member. If you use plywood for the doors, you do not need to frame the doors unless you want the framing for a design effect. The back of the plywood panels will be smooth, possibly with a few tight knots.

Backs of storage doors also can be used for storage, providing this doesn't put too much weight on the doors. These doors are constructed from 4- by 8-foot sheets of A/A fir plywood (the plywood is quality veneer on both sides—free from knots and large imperfections). The framing can be 1- by 4- or 1- by 6-inch members screwed (or nailed) to the plywood in simple butt joints. The narrow shelves are nailed to the edge members; the ¾-inch plywood inserts for trays and lids also are nailed at an angle to the edge members. You can use regular butt hinges on the doors; if the doors will support a lot of weight, use continuous (piano) hinges. (See continuous hinges in Index.) The basic shelving in this cabinet is fixed, although adjustable shelving can be used.

A series of adjustable shelves forms this storage wall which has been especially tailored to fit the refrigerator. The supporting vertical members may be hardwood-faced plywood ($^3/_4$ inch thick). The edges of the plywood are finished with 1- by 2-inch members to add dimension to the plywood, or for design purposes the vertical framing could be 2- by 12-inch lumber.

SIMPLE CABINETS AND SHELVES WITH A FLAIR

Most storage units involve simple boxlike cabinets you can buy or build from standard plywood and boards purchased at home center stores and building material retailers. Your toughest task may be choosing the right storage design to solve those storage problems.

Regular prefabricated cabinets, most often used as kitchen cabinets, are manufactured in a variety of sizes, styles, and finishes. The cabinets are usually 24 inches deep and 34 inches high. With a 2-inch top, the total height of the cabinet becomes standard—36 inches high. The height can be modified, of course, to suit your design.

Standard wall cabinets are 12 inches deep and from 12 to 36 inches high. The widths start at 9 inches and range to 36 inches. You also may buy fillers for both base and wall cabinets which are used to space out odd dimensions.

If you don't purchase stock cabinets and you don't want to build your own cabinets, you can have the cabinets built by a custom millwork company, but these are more expensive. Do not settle on one millwork shop for your project until you have bids from several other shops. This business is highly competitive; you may be able to get a better price by comparative shopping.

A door to nowhere? Older homes have lots of doorways, many of which are nonfunctional. If this is the case in your home, here's an idea for extra storage space: seal off one side of the passageway and use it for attractive bookshelves. The bottom shelf matches the height of the baseboard, an additional piece of matching baseboard will have to be used as a filler. Adjustable shelf brackets may be used at the side jambs of the door to support the shelves. To carry out the shelving design, make a simple rectangle of 1- by 5-inch boards, and hinge this rectangle to the side jambs—just as you would a door. The same casing may be used.

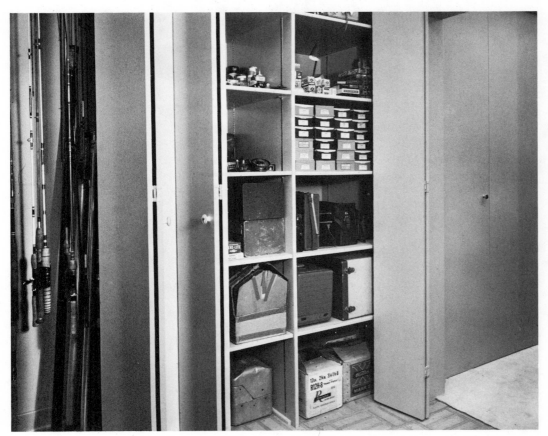

This sports storage center is a simple eggcrate design of shelving measured to fit a specific closet space. The shelving may be plywood or 1- by 12-inch boards butt-joined, screwed, and glued together. Adjustable shelf brackets permit flexibility within the cabinet although fixed shelving may be used instead. The bifold doors run on a standard track which is attached to a framing header at the front of the closet wall.

Right:
Both adjustable and sliding shelving make up this storage nook for seldom-used items such as luggage and kitchenware. The design and construction are extremely simple: vertical support members for the shelving are fitted into available closet space. The entire unit may be fabricated in a workshop and simply installed in the closet. You can buy sliding tray hardware at most home center and building material stores. The hardware is screwed to the side of the shelves and to the vertical members.

Far right:
"Growth" closet for youngsters starts small and grows as the kids get older. Closet poles are designed for current and out-of-season storage; the unit shown here is a plywood insert cut to fit the closet dimensions. When the kids are older, the insert may be removed and a standard closet design used.

Look to the ceiling for storage when rooms are cramped. This unit (see the following photograph) looks like a dropped or suspended ceiling. The bottom is tiled with ceiling tile that matches the tile on the rest of the ceiling in the room.

Pull down on the suspended ceiling and the ceiling becomes a model train table. The table may be constructed from 4- by 8- by ³/₄-inch plywood tiled on one side. Edging, which adds thickness to the table and provides a niche for the tile, can be 1- by 3-inch boards nailed or screwed and glued to the plywood edges. The cables hooked to eyebolts at each corner or the plywood are counterbalanced in the attic crawl space above. You also may buy spring-loaded cable mechanisms at hardware stores for this type installation.

Simple hardwood-faced plywood boxes make up this home study center. A single sheet of plywood covered with high-pressure laminate forms the desk top; the drawer is suspended from the top. The television stand is castered so it can be moved within the room; the front of this cabinet is the same plywood as the other cabinets. The shelves ride on standard adjustable shelf brackets.

Unfinished furniture may be used for this study/storage center. The furniture pieces sit on a rectangular base of 2 by 4s; the shelves are simple rectangles of 1- by 12-inch lumber with matching shelves that sit on adjustable shelving brackets. The top is high-pressure laminate cemented to a 3/4-inch plywood core. The top is then screwed on from underneath the cabinets.

Telephone center storage is cut from between the wall studs. First the gypsum board was removed from the wall. Then a simple box of 1- by 4-inch pine boards was assembled with nails and glue. The box is backed with a piece of 1/8-inch plywood. The box was inserted into the slot in the wall and nailed to the studs.

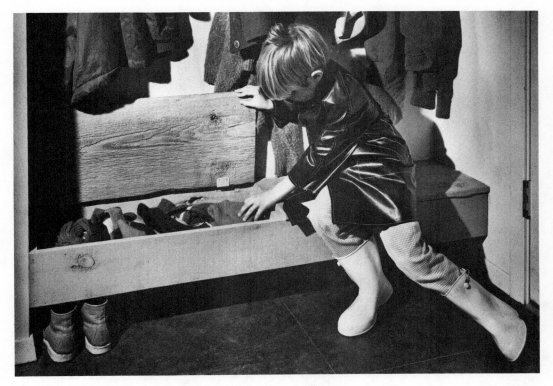

Open closet in utility area features a low bench with a compartment for gloves and scarves. For added support, the bench can be framed with 2- by 4-inch framing members. Cover the members with plywood, or use 1 by 8s for members which are nailed to the studs. The bench top can be 1- by 12-inch boards; if you want a wider bench top, you will have to cut the top from a piece of plywood. Use semiconcealed hinges to fasten the top to the framing members.

Simple shelving for any room can be spaced with rectangular boxes of plywood, as shown, or with concrete blocks or bricks. These boxes are covered with contact paper for design purposes but can be painted, wallpapered, or covered with a high-pressure laminate. The shelves are 2- by 12-inch boards stained to match the box covering.

For large families, this schoolhouse cloakroom rack is ideal for the kids' coats and lunch boxes and anything else you want to keep from being underfoot. The rack is fastened through its back to the wall studs with wood screws; the height is adjustable depending on the size of the children.

Dividers in the rack are cut from 1- by 8-inch material and fastened to the bottom member with wood screws. The 1- by 2-inch board along the bottom edge of the rack helps to support the rack on the wall and to give design dimension to the entire unit, which can be any length you want. Regular coat hooks are spaced along the bottom board, and the hooks are set about 12 inches apart although they may be at any spacing.

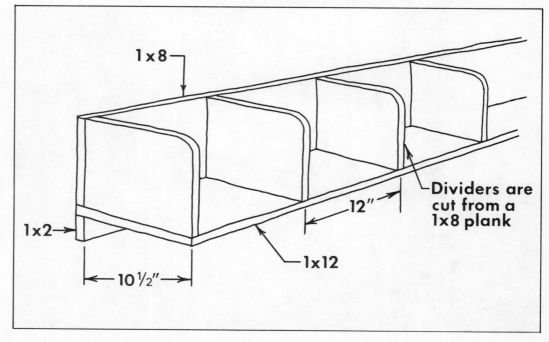

1×8

1×2

12"

Dividers are cut from a 1×8 plank

1×12

10½"

This simple, four-sided box offers a decorative feature as well as storage for dishes. The box simply sits on a shelf and can be used to store small plates and/ or saucers. Use 1- by 6- or 1- by 8-inch material for the box; the butt joints are nailed or screwed together and glued.

Understair storage can be a series of cabinets and drawers or just one large cabinet with one door. The layout for cabinets and drawers is a complex one, but the framing for this setup can be done in sections so that everything fits perfectly. (See drawer and cabinet framing in Index.) If you use just one door for the storage unit, you can frame the space with 2- by 4-inch studs and cover it with paneling or gypsum wallboard. The door may be attached to the framing like any regular door unit, or the space may be left open and a series of shelf units installed for storage.

WINE RACKS

This handsome wine rack is nothing more than two parallel 2 by 8s spaced 6 inches apart with holes especially aligned to support the bottles at a slight angle. Since the neck of a wine bottle is smaller than its base, the holes may be bored in a series. Align the bottom edges of the holes on both 2 by 8s, spacing them exactly. The smaller holes are 1 inch in diameter; the larger holes are 5 inches in diameter. Unless you have the equipment, we suggest you have a millwork shop bore the holes for you.

Three 1- by 8-inch spacer blocks hold the 2 by 8s apart and serve to hold the wine rack against the wall. The unit goes together with flathead screws and glue. The screws are counterbored, and the holes are plugged with dowels. (See dowels in Index.) The unit is fastened to the wall studs or wall with screws or toggle bolts; the holes for the fasteners are counterbored and plugged with dowels. Since the bottles are tipped at a slight angle, they will not fall out of the holes.

This built-in wine cabinet could also be freestanding, if you don't have space for the depth of the cabinet in another room. In either type, the racks have two parallel 1- by 5-inch members that are notched to hold the base and necks of the bottles. These members are fastened to the framing members of the cabinet. This same cabinet without the doors can be modified for a basement location.

LAWN, GARDEN, AND WORKSHOP STORAGE

Nifty lawn and garden equipment storage utilizes about 6 inches of deck space and blends in with the deck when closed. Two 2 by 8s hinged at the bottom of a 4-foot span simply fold down so hoses, shears, chemical containers, and so forth may be stored behind them. A friction catch at the top of the sections holds the doors in position against a 2- by 10-inch top sill. The sill is held in place by two fixed, short sections of 2 by 8s at either end of the span. The length of the doors can be any measurement.

A home workshop is the ideal spot for perforated hardboard storage. By lining the walls with perforated hardboard and then painting the material a light-reflecting color, you not only have a spot to store tools but a brighter room in which to work. In the basement use tempered hardboard, which is moisture resistant. Standard hardboard may be used anywhere there is not a moisture problem. Perforated hardboard has to be furred out from the wall with strips of 1 by 2s or 1 by 3s. The space between the back of the hardboard and the wall permits hooks to be inserted in the hardboard. You don't need much furring—usually a strip at the top and bottom of the panel and another strip centered between these two strips will provide sufficient support.

Between-the-studs storage is also ideal for a workshop since the space doesn't rob you of valuable floor space. Remove a section of gypsum wallboard between studs (you may have to remove one stud to have a larger area), and use adjustable brackets to support the 1- by 3-inch shelves. A bifold or standard door is optional.

CUSTOMIZE STANDARD STORAGE CABINETS

Building materials are milled and manufactured in modules. Standard modules are 2 feet, 4 feet, 8 feet, 16 feet.

Your home or apartment is built on a module. For example, wall studs, rafters, and joists are on 16-inch centers. Three studs or rafters represent 48 inches—or 4 feet. Most wall-covering materials—paneling and gypsum wallboard—are 4 feet wide to fit this measurement.

Cabinets, too, are made on modules. It is best to use these modules when you build or buy storage cabinets and shelving, either as finished or as raw materials. You generally get a price break on modular materials over specially cut materials. For example, if you need a 4- by 6-foot piece of plywood,

the piece will have to be cut from a piece of 4- by 8-foot plywood. You pay for the larger piece, plus the cutting, plus the scrap piece, which may or may not be usable.

By far the easiest storage to construct consists of prefabricated and prefinished cabinets and shelving. Assembly and installation are kept to a minimum, and the project looks good since there is little margin for error.

Basic kitchen cabinets may be used in any room in your home since there is a wide variety of styles from which to choose. These cabinets may be modified by adding shelves, trays, and dividers to suit your storage needs. The modification usually is an easy job, often requiring no more than several pieces of hardboard or plywood to create the tailored space.

Sliding trays replace shelving in this kitchen base cabinet. The trays are in a "U" configuration, and they are made from ¾-inch plywood panels. The sliding tray hardware is standard; you may buy it at most home center and hardware stores. Installation instructions are on the packaging.

A wooden box, for holding additional utensils, is also fabricated from plywood and is attached to the sliding tray. The box is fastened to the tray top with small angle braces from the inside to keep the box from moving or tipping. You can use dividers in the box to keep the utensils separated.

This bathroom cabinet, recessed in the wall between the studs, is covered with custom-made mirrors which form a wall of reflection. The mirrors are set in a framework of 1 by 4s grooved to accept the mirror glass. The doors are hinged to 1- by 2-inch framing (dividing) members; these members are nailed to the wall studs. Magnetic catches hold the mirror frames shut.

A standard base cabinet with a drop leaf, butcher block top is a handy, functional addition to any kitchen. Three sections of butcher block are hinged together with continuous (piano) hinges; the drop leaves are held with regular drop leaf brackets attached to the side of the cabinet and to the bottom of the blocks. The main top is anchored to the cabinet with screws driven from underneath the regular cabinet top. Casters have been added to the base of the cabinet to give it more mobility and versatility.

Right:
Laundry storage is handier when baskets of clothing slide out of their closets on washday. The closet is fabricated from standard interior grade ¾-inch plywood; the trays also are ¾-inch plywood mounted on sliding tray hardware.

Far right:
Wide laundry trays located under a countertop between a base cabinet and wall offer ample laundry storage. The trays are ¾-inch panels of plywood edged with 1- by 3-inch boards for extra design dimension and support. The 1- by 3-inch side members also support the sliding tray hardware which is fastened to both the members and to sides of the cabinet and wall.

SIMPLE STORAGE FOR SEWING CENTERS

Wall and base cabinets make this a smoothly running sewing center. The base cabinets can be pieces of unfinished furniture. A common countertop, laminated with high-pressure plastic, is fastened to the tops of the cabinets to form a single unit. The wall cabinets have adjustable shelving; a wide base provides a light baffle. Because of its evenness, fluorescent lighting is used beneath the wall cabinets.

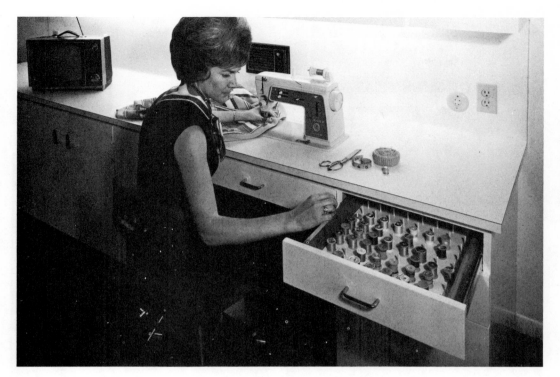

Drawers are customized with dowel pegs which hold spools of thread. Customizing is easy to do by drilling a series of holes in a piece of ⅝-inch plywood cut to fit the drawer bottom. The dowels are inserted into the holes with glue.

Utility storage next to the sewing center has sliding tray shelves. The cabinet is an eggcrate design with simple plywood doors hinged to the framing. The countertop for the sewing machine may double as a desk.

Carefully Planned Storage   27

LITTLE TOUCHES THAT MEAN A LOT

Right:
Otherwise wasted space was utilized at the side of this range with a small, narrow base cabinet. The cabinet is a simple rectangle of ¾-inch hardwood-faced plywood, glued and nailed together. The door and drawer fronts are flush panels; the door swings on semiconcealed hinges that require only a saw kerf for installation.

Far right:
Cooking utensils are kept in the drawer, handy to the range; lids and trays are kept in the door section of the cabinet. The homemaker also has the advantage of having a small countertop; the top may be covered with ceramic tile or other heat-proof material so hot pans may be placed on it while food is being prepared.

Space around a refrigerator is usually wasted or at best disorganized since the size of the refrigerator determines the size of the cabinets that surround it.

COORDINATED STORAGE IDEAS

An end storage unit puts this wasted space to good use and organizes food storage. The cabinet and door storage is one can deep. The shelves operate on adjustable shelf brackets, and the door, because of its weight, swings on a continuous (piano) hinge. Hardwood-faced plywood is used for the cabinet. There is no other framing, except 2-by 4-inch members fastened to the floor. The cabinet is fastened to these members and to one end of the kitchen wall cabinets.

Right:
Between-the-studs kitchen wall storage also is one can deep—the width of a 2-by 4-inch stud. The shelves are fixed on 1- by 2-inch shelf supports; the door is ¾-inch plywood edged with solid wood trim for design. The front of the door is used as a bulletin board. The door does not fit flush with the wall surface; the trim slightly overlaps the opening, creating a raised panel effect.

Far right:
Odd-dimension space, again alongside a refrigerator, was put to use by this homeowner. The cabinet is fabricated from plywood; the edges are trimmed with solid wood. The door is fastened to the side of the cabinet with a continuous hinge, and by installing a false floor in the bottom of the cabinet, you create regular kitchen cabinet "toe room."

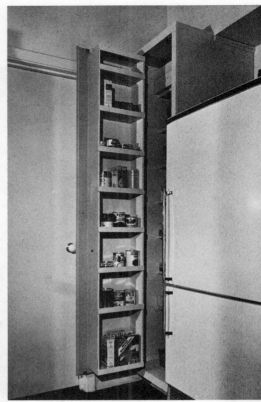

Kitchen storage doesn't have to be confined to cabinets. Here's a large brass curtain rod that has been adapted with eyes and hooks to support fancy skillets and cooking pans. Besides freeing cabinet space, the rod/utensil combination provides a decorative aspect in the kitchen. The hardware is available at home center and hardware stores.

Smartly styled shelving can serve as a storage facility as well as a room divider. These shelves are in a tray design. The bottoms are 1 by 6s; the sides and ends are 1 by 3s. Pick a select hardwood for the shelving—walnut, maple, oak—since the shelves are visible.

Special storage for flatware is easy to create within a cabinet by using plywood dividers that fit into slots (dadoes). If you don't have a power saw to cut the slots, you can fabricate them with small pieces of molding. (See molding in Index.) The storage at right has plastic baskets mounted on sliding tray hardware.

Linens stay neater when they are stored over closet poles, as shown. The brackets for the poles may be made from $^5/_4$-inch lumber or 2 by 4s. (See brackets in Index.) You also can buy closet pole hardware to support the poles. If the pole must bear a lot of weight, consider using ¾-inch galvanized steel pipe for the poles and regular pipe flanges for the supports. The flanges are screwed onto the ends of the pipe and then to the wall framing member.

Tools and Materials for Building Basic Storage Units

You do not have to invest heavily in tools and equipment to build basic storage units. There are, however, several tools that you must have for jobs as simple as installing shelving or setting base and wall cabinets. Chances are you have these basic tools already. If not, look at the expenditure as twofold:

1. You can use the tools to build storage.

2. You can use the tools for regular home maintenance chores that come up often: repairing loose and broken siding, fixing gutters, and repairing screens and storm windows.

These basic tools and their approximate costs are as follows:

- 13- or 16-ounce claw hammer ($10)
- Crosscut saw ($9)
- Miter box and backsaw ($10)
- Screwdriver set (standard and Phillips) ($8)
- Block plane ($10)
- Combination square ($8)
- 25-foot tape measure ($6)
- Chisel set ($12)
- Keyhole saw ($6)
- Multipurpose smoothing plane ($5)
- Drill set ($8)
- Pliers ($2)
- Razor knife ($1)
- Level ($12)

We have purposely left power tools off the equipment list, mainly because this is a book about basic techniques.

Of course, power equipment will speed any wood-working project. Yet the basic tools will give you professional-looking results without the expenditure for power tools at the outset. Too, you can buy many prefabricated storage parts at home center stores and building material outlets. By doing so, you eliminate the need for fancy cuts and joining techniques that require power tools.

If, however, you are considering power tools for your workshop, we suggest these basic ones:

- 10-inch bench saw
- Portable electric sabre saw
- ¼-inch or ⅜-inch portable electric drill

A word about buying tools

Do not invest your money in *cheap* tools. Good quality tools cost just a few dollars more and will last a lifetime if you care for them properly.

A good tool will have well-machined parts. The tools will feel well balanced when you handle them, not awkward or clumsy. Handles and striking surfaces will be rugged but well machined. In short, the tools will look and feel as if they will do the job they are supposed to do.

The same quality message applies to power equipment, too. The cheap equipment will quickly break down under normal use.

MATERIALS: PLYWOOD, LUMBER, AND BOARDS

Most of your storage projects will require basic materials with which to work including boards, lumber, plywood, hardboard, and moldings.

Boards are lengths of lumber that are 1 inch thick in nominal size. For example, the dimension may be 1 by 2, 1 by 3, 1 by 4, and so forth. (See the chart in this chapter for standard lumber sizes.)

Dimension lumber is lumber that is 2 inches thick in nominal size. For example, 2 by 4, 2 by 6, and 2 by 8.

There are two kinds of boards and lumber: softwood and hardwood.

Softwood refers to hemlock, fir, pine, spruce, cypress, and redwood. In building storage space, you probably will use pine most often since it is easy to work with using the basic hand tools, and it takes stain or paint beautifully. The second choice probably will be fir. It, too, is fairly easy to work with in general construction using hand tools. Softwoods are used for framing and in other places where the wood won't show.

Hardwood refers to mahogany, walnut, oak, maple, and birch. Hardwood is expensive, and, therefore, you will want to use it for cabinets and trims.

Boards and lumber are especially graded according to two basic classifications: *common lumber,* which has defects and is used for construction and general-purpose building projects; and *select lumber,* which is sound and of good quality and is used when appearance is important.

The grades of common lumber are: No. 1, which contains only a few tight knots and blemishes and is suitable for painting; No. 2, which has larger knots and blemishes and can also be painted or used for flooring and paneling; No. 3, which has loose knots and flaws and should be used for shelving or where the wood won't show; No. 4, which is an economy grade and should be used only for subflooring, crating, sheeting, and concrete forms.

The grades of select lumber are: B and better (or 1 and 2 clear), which has only tiny imperfections; C select grade, which has limited imperfections; D select grade, which has many imperfections and is sometimes sold covered by a coat of paint to hide the defects.

Lumber is sold by the board foot. A board foot is a piece of lumber that is 1 inch think, 12 inches wide, and 12 inches long. Don't worry about computing the board feet; the lumber retailer will compute it for you.

Basic lumber sizes

Lumber type	Nominal size (in inches)	Actual size (in inches) (Wood is surfaced on four sides and is kiln dried.)
Boards	1 x 2	¾ x 1½
	1 x 3	¾ x 2½
	1 x 4	¾ x 3½
	1 x 5	¾ x 4½
	1 x 6	¾ x 5½
	1 x 7	¾ x 6½
	1 x 8	¾ x 7½
Dimension	2 x 4	1½ x 3½
	2 x 6	1½ x 5½
	2 x 8	1½ x 7¼
	2 x 10	1¼ x 9¼

Plywood

Plywood sheets are available in two faces: hardwood-faced and softwood-faced. Hardwood faces include oak, mahogany, cherry, birch, and walnut, and softwood faces include fir, pine, and spruce.

Most plywood is subjected to industry grading standards which assure you that material purchased is uniform. There are standards that permit plugging knotholes and mending split voids. This doesn't mean that the material is of inferior quality; instead it assures that you get what you pay for.

Most plywood which is readily available today is graded by the American Plywood Association and bears a back stamp or edgemark on the panel. This mark is your assurance that the plywood has been manufactured to the

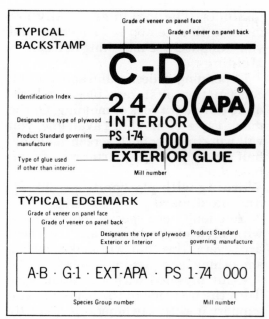

TYPICAL BACKSTAMP

Grade of veneer on panel face
Grade of veneer on panel back

C-D
24/0 **APA**
INTERIOR
Identification Index
Designates the type of plywood
Product Standard governing
manufacture
PS 1-74
000
Type of glue used
if other than interior
EXTERIOR GLUE
Mill number

TYPICAL EDGEMARK
Grade of veneer on panel face
Grade of veneer on panel back
Designates the type of plywood
Exterior or Interior
Product Standard
governing manufacture

A-B · G-1 · EXT·APA · PS 1·74 000

Species Group number   Mill number

quality standards and performance requirements of the association.

The following grading information is designed to give you some working knowledge when talking to your plywood dealer. With his help you can select the plywood best suited to your project and your budget.

Hardwood-faced plywood is graded differently from softwood-faced.

Hardwood-faced comes in interior type, which is moisture resistant, and exterior, which is waterproof. It is further defined according to veneer grades: the better the grade, the more expensive the material.

A Premium
1 Good
2 Sound
3 Utility
4 Backing
SP Specialty grade (which has unusual decorative features)

Some general considerations of hardwood-faced plywood: it is used primarily as paneling or as facing material in the ¼-inch thickness and for construction of furniture or cabinets in the ¾-inch thickness; hardwood-faced plywood is often prefinished.

Although you can build cabinets from hardwood-faced plywood you might consider a less expensive frame with a hardwood plywood facing or use softwood-faced plywood, which is usually less expensive, and apply your own finish.

Softwood-faced plywood is also manufactured in exterior and interior. These two types are further identified according to appearance by veneer grades, and according to stiffness and strength by groups.

Exterior plywood is 100% waterproof and is suited to permanent outdoor applications and those subject to continuing moist conditions or extremely high humidity. Interior plywood is highly moisture resistant and is well suited for storage projects.

Veneer grades are designated according to the appearance quality of the face and back veneer and are indicated by letters:

N Special order "natural finish" veneer; select all hardwood or all sapwood; free of open defects; allows some repairs. (This grade is in limited supply and is very expensive.)

A Smooth and paintable; neatly made repairs permissable.

B Solid surface veneer; circular and other nontapered repair plugs and tight knots permitted.

C Knotholes and limited splits permitted; minimum veneer permitted in exterior-type plywood.

C-Plugged Improved C veneer with splits limited to ⅛-inch in width and knotholes and borer holes limited to ¼-inch by ½-inch.

D Permits knots and knotholes to 2½-inches in width and ½-inch larger under certain specified limits; limited splits permitted.

Where the plywood will show, consider A or B veneers; when appearance is not important, use C, C-plugged, or D.

Softwood plywood is designated by group to indicate its stiffness and strength and the species of wood it contains. The groups range from 1 through 5 with the stiffest and strongest woods in Group 1.

Similarities between hardwood-faced

and softwood-faced plywoods include grade combinations, glue bonds, and thicknesses. You can buy veneer grade combinations so that when the face will show and the backing won't, you can choose a 1 front and 3 back in hardwood-faced plywood or an A front and C back in softwood-faced plywood. Also, in general, the glue bonds of both faces are classified as waterproof, water resistant, and dry. Even if you buy an interior plywood (hardwood or softwood), you may want a waterproof bond if the plywood is being used in a place with high humidity. Thicknesses of hardwood-faced and softwood-faced plywood are: $1/4, 3/8, 1/2, 5/8, 3/4$ and 1 inch.

Hardboard for storage

Hardboard is really wood. The material is made from wood chips that are turned into sheets under heat and pressure.

There are two types of hardboard: standard and tempered. If moisture is not a problem, use standard; tempered hardboard has been treated to withstand moisture.

Hardboard makes excellent sliding cabinet doors, drawer bottoms, and special decorative inserts, and it is lower-priced than plywood.

When working with hardboard, remember this: hardboard is grainless. Therefore, hardboard has to be fastened to wood framing members. You can't fasten wood to hardboard. That is, you can't nail or screw a piece of trim to the hardboard; you have to nail or screw the hardboard to the trim.

Sizes of hardboard panels range from 4 by 4 to 4 by 16 feet. The standard sizes are 4- by 8- and 4- by 10-foot panels. Thicknesses are $1/8, 3/16, 1/4,$ and $5/16$ inch.

There is a wide range of hardboard panels with embossed designs. The embossing is so realistic that it is difficult to tell the product from real hardwood-faced plywood. You may be able to use these panels to face some storage projects, remembering that the panels have to be fastened to a framework.

Hardboard manufacturers also provide various moldings and trim for their products. The moldings usually are metal with an embossed covering, and you can purchase matching nails.

Moldings

Depending on design and application, construction of storage pieces will require different types of molding. Of the many types of moldings available, you will work mostly with screen molding, half round, ply cap, quarter round, and base shoe.

Working with plywood and hardboard

You don't need special tools to work with plywood or hardboard, but here are several tips that will make sawing, smoothing, and planing easier.

• Cut plywood with a crosscut saw. Turn the best side of the panel up, and support it with sawhorses or a sturdy table so the saw doesn't bind in the saw kerf.

• If you cut plywood with a power saw, turn the best side of the panel down. Use a crosscut blade or a combination blade.

• When planing plywood, start from the ends and run the plane toward the center of the panel to prevent splitting at corners and edges.

• Always sand plywood in the direction of the grain. Stretch the sandpaper over a sanding block, and don't apply too much pressure, which tends to "dig" the top veneer, or sand too much, which can cut through the thin top veneer.

• If possible, never drive a nail or screw into the edge of plywood; this can split the veneer. If you have to use a fastener, drill a pilot hole first.

• Saw hardboard with a crosscut saw. If you use a power saw, use a combination or crosscut blade, or a carbide-tipped blade. Hardboard is extremely tough and dulls sawblades quickly.

• When drilling holes in hardboard, work from the "finished" side of the sheet.

• Hardboard must be supported by framing members such as 2 by 4s. In installations where panels are used, support the panels every 16 inches.

• Before installing hardboard or plywood in damp exterior storage, cover the walls adjoining the panels with a moisture-vaporproof barrier such as polyethylene film.

• Hardboard panels, such as those used in drawer bottoms, should "float."

Do not fasten the panels securely; hardboard tends to absorb moisture and expand. Leave a little space for this expansion, and the contraction that may later result.

BOARD AND LUMBER MEASUREMENTS

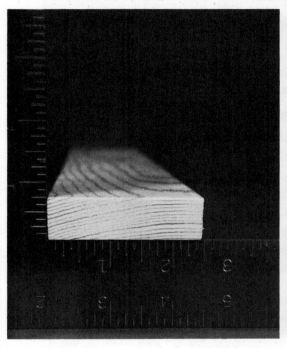 

Left:
Boards have a nominal size of 1 by 2, 1 by 3, 1 by 4, and so on. (See chart.) The actual size of boards differs, however. For example, a 1 by 2 measures ¾ by 1½ inches. This picture shows a piece of 1 by 3. As you can see, it measures ¾ by 2½ inches. Take this into consideration when you design and lay out your storage project.

Far left:
Dimension lumber also has a nominal and actual size. This is a piece whose nominal size is 2 by 4, but it actually measures 1½ by 3½ inches. Both boards and dimension lumber may be slightly off in measurement because of the moisture content of the wood. A lot of moisture tends to swell the wood slightly; low humidity tends to shrink the wood.

Five/quarter (⁵/₄) lumber actually measures a full inch thick by whatever width you want up to 12 inches. Because of its thickness, ⁵/₄ stock is an excellent choice for shelving and provides design considerations that thinner material doesn't.

Veneer-core plywood has three inner plies. Top and bottom veneers are bonded to these plies. The grains of the veneers alternate at right angles to give the panels more strength. For exterior storage projects, use exterior-type plywood; for interior projects, use interior-type plywood with a water-resistant glue bond.

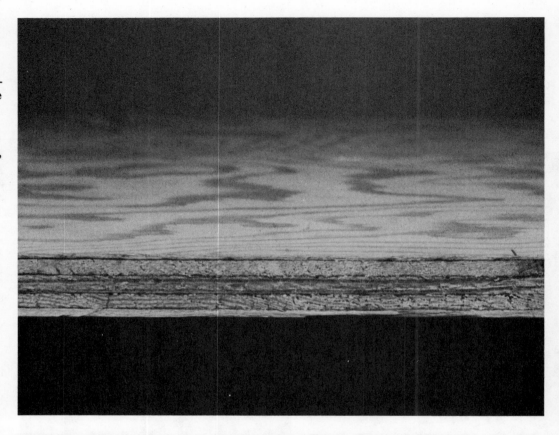

Particle board-core plywood is either veneered on both sides of the core or veneered on one side and sanded smooth on the other. You also can buy particle board without veneer. Particle board is made from wood chips that are resin coated and is very dense and heavy. Like hardboard, particle board should be nailed to framing members; do not nail framing members to it unless the particle board has a veneer finish. Particle board is dimensionally stable and is a good material for cabinets.

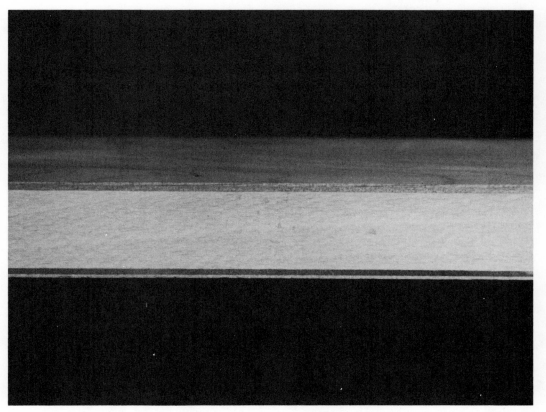

Lumber-core plywood has sheets of veneer laminated to a core of solid wood and is especially suitable for cabinets, since the core is extremely strong and laminated for stress. The edges of lumber-core plywood are very easy to finish and take mortising and fasteners better than veneer-core or particle board-core panels.

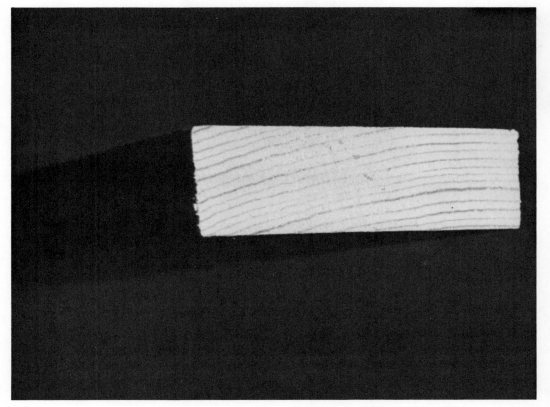

Flat-grained boards and lumber are stronger than their vertical-grained counterparts; the grain runs across the width of the board. Always select this material for storage framing.

Although flat-grained boards and lumber are stronger than vertical-grained material, they may warp and shrink when exposed to a lot of moisture or humidity. Always buy kiln-dried boards and lumber for storage projects. They cost more but tend to remain stable without developing checks or splitting, bowing, twisting, and cupping.

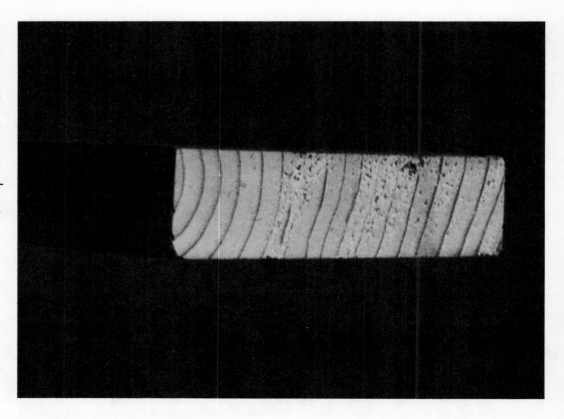

FASTENERS FOR STORAGE

Almost any storage project has to be assembled and fastened together. The most common fasteners you will use are nails, screws, and glue. Special types of fasteners are wiggle nails, plugs, anchors, metal plates, and brackets.

Nails

The nail should be 3 times longer than the thickness of the board or lumber you are nailing. If you are working with thin and thick pieces of material—such as ¼-inch thick plywood and 2- by 4-inch framing—always try to fasten the thin piece to the thicker piece, so that two-thirds of the nail will be in the thicker piece. Drive nails into wood at an angle; this makes them hold better.

Nails are manufactured from aluminum, copper, brass, stainless steel, bronze, and Monel metals. Common nails are used for framing or rough-in carpentry jobs; finishing nails are for trim and cabinet projects; casing nails are similar to finishing nails but are heavier in body; ring or ring-shanked nails are for extra holding power.

Screws

The screw used to fasten materials together should be, like the nail, 3 times longer than the thickness of the material. Screw sizes are numbered according to length and gauge (thickness): a No. 16 wood screw, for example, is 2½ inches long. Lengths range from ¼ inch to 6 inches, and the sizes are usually approximate.

Screw types include oval head and flathead screws, which are countersunk (recessed) below the surface of the material, and roundhead screws, which are not countersunk. There are two basic slot types: plain slotted, which requires a standard blade screwdriver, and Phillips slotted, for which you use a Phillips screwdriver.

You can buy decorative washers for the screws that will show on cabinets. Washers provide more bearing surface for the screwheads and help prevent marring of the wood when screws are driven or drawn.

Common screw sizes

Gauge	Length	Gauge	Length
No. 2	¼ to ½ inch	No. 10	⅝ to 2¼ inches
No. 3	¼ to ⅝ inch	No. 12	⅞ to 2½ inches
No. 4	⅜ to ¾ inch	No. 14	1 to 2¾ inches
No. 5	⅜ to ¾ inch	No. 16	1¼ to 3 inches
No. 6	⅜ to 1½ inches	No. 18	1½ to 4 inches
No. 7	⅜ to 1½ inches	No. 20	1¾ to 4 inches
No. 8	½ to 2 inches	No. 24	3½ to 4 inches
No. 9	⅝ to 2¼ inches		

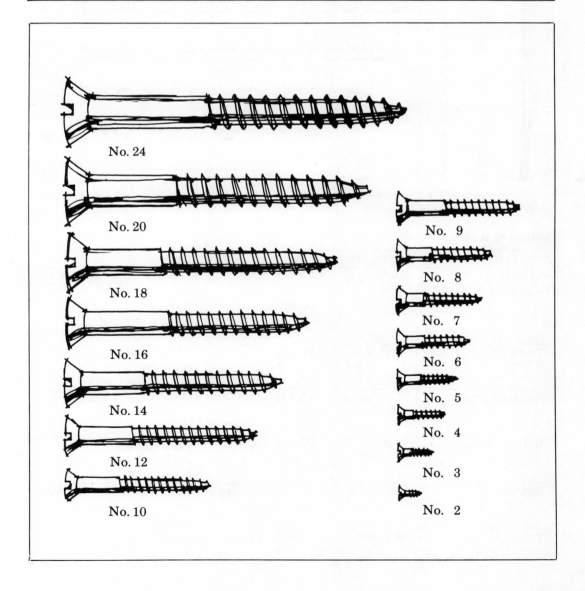

No. 24

No. 20

No. 18

No. 16

No. 14

No. 12

No. 10

No. 9

No. 8

No. 7

No. 6

No. 5

No. 4

No. 3

No. 2

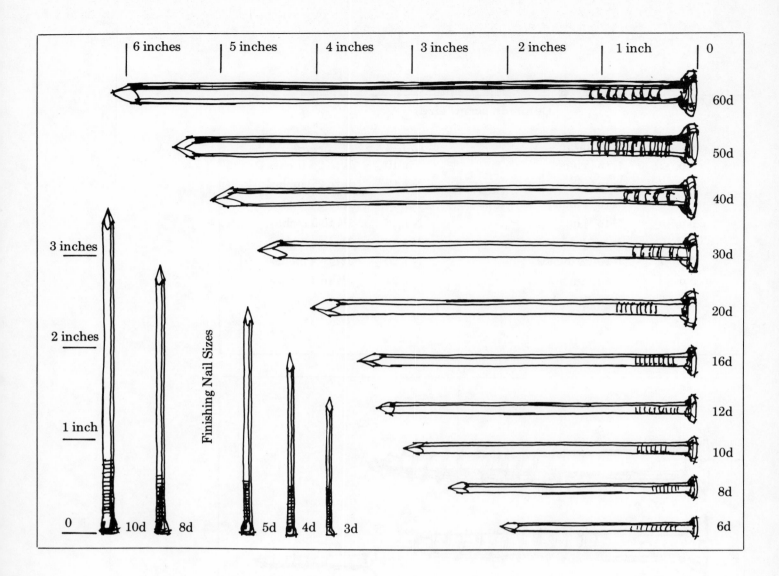

Finishing Nail Sizes

Adhesive fasteners

Type of adhesive	Drying time	Use	Data
Aliphatic resin	Fast	Wood	Water resistant
Animal or fish	Slow	Wood, paper	Little moisture or heat resistance; brittle when dry and aged
Casein	Medium	Wood, fabrics	Good heat resistance; poor moisture resistance
Casein or latex	Medium	Metal, glass, fabric, plastic	Good heat/water resistance
Thermoplastic	Fast	Wood, paper, plastics	May damage rubber, plastic, and lacquer finishes
Contact	Fast	Joining plastic laminate to wood	Ideal for cabinetmaking; resistant to heat and water
Epoxy	Medium	Wood, china, metal	Won't shrink; holds tightly

Working with adhesives

• Sand wood joints lightly before applying adhesive. Sanding will open the grain of the wood, giving the adhesive more holding power. Make sure the joints are square; the more the surfaces touch, the better the glue bond will be.

• Clamp the glue joint, if possible. Do not squeeze the joint too tightly with the clamp; tighten the clamp with finger pressure only.

• Use a filler-type glue, if you can't clamp the joint.

STORAGE DIMENSIONS

We can't tell you what size storage unit or shelving to build. But we can give you some dimension basics that may help you determine what you can put in the space you have. When measuring, use a rule, not a wooden yardstick.

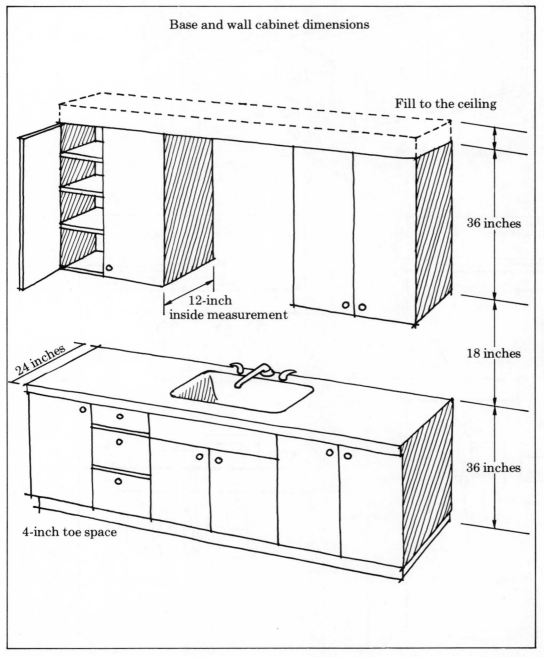

Base and wall cabinet dimensions

Fill to the ceiling

36 inches

12-inch inside measurement

24 inches

18 inches

36 inches

4-inch toe space

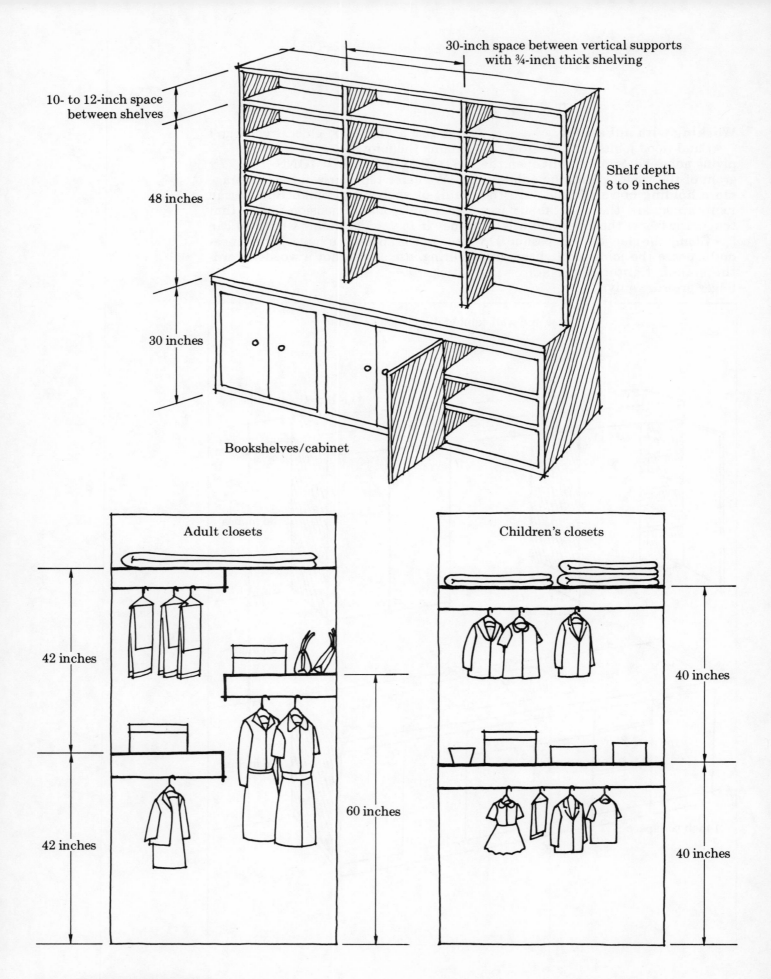

30-inch space between vertical supports with ¾-inch thick shelving

10- to 12-inch space between shelves

48 inches

Shelf depth 8 to 9 inches

30 inches

Bookshelves/cabinet

Adult closets

42 inches

42 inches

60 inches

Children's closets

40 inches

40 inches

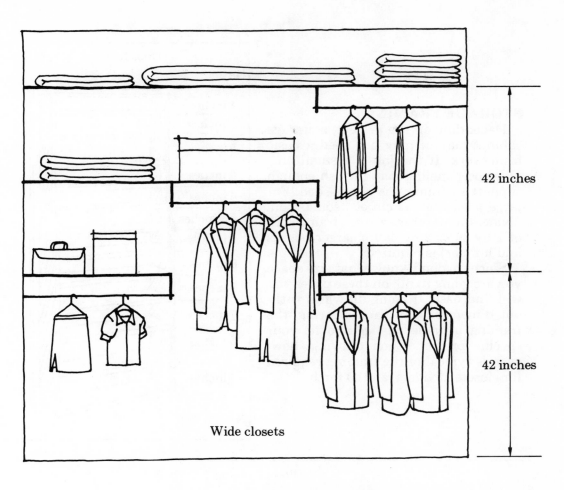

42 inches

42 inches

Wide closets

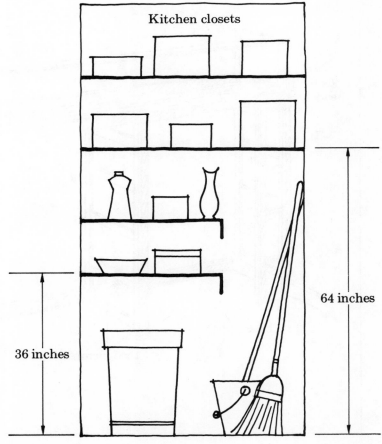

Kitchen closets

64 inches

36 inches

STORAGE FRAMING

Depending on the project, a storage cabinet may or may not need a basic framework. If the job is a small one, plywood paneling may furnish enough support so framing is not needed. For large jobs, such as closets, some room dividers, and storage walls, a framework of 1 by 4s or 2 by 4s (or larger boards and lumber) is required.

Since we don't know what size space you are going to fill, on these pages you will find basic framing drawings without dimensions. In each drawing, the framing may be changed to fit your specific project. Each drawing, however, is typical of the framing required for closets, dividers, and so forth.

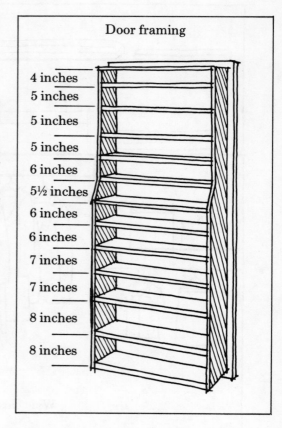

Door framing

4 inches
5 inches
5 inches
5 inches
6 inches
5½ inches
6 inches
6 inches
7 inches
7 inches
8 inches
8 inches

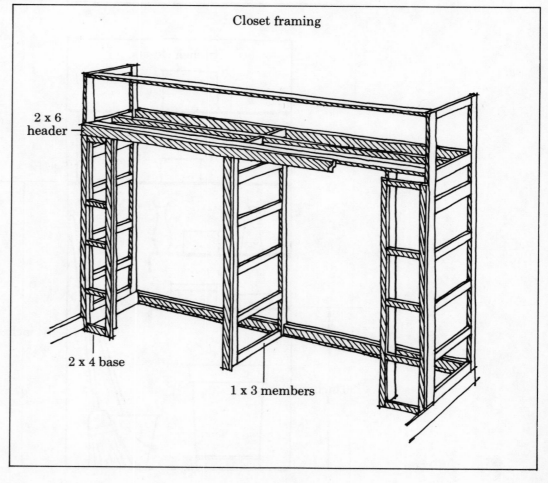

Closet framing

2 x 6 header

2 x 4 base

1 x 3 members

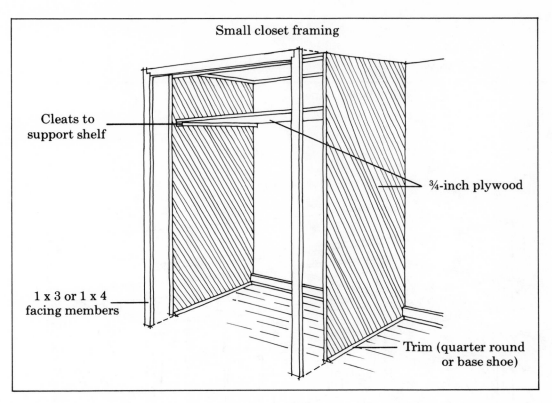

Small closet framing

Cleats to
support shelf

¾-inch plywood

1 x 3 or 1 x 4
facing members

Trim (quarter round
or base shoe)

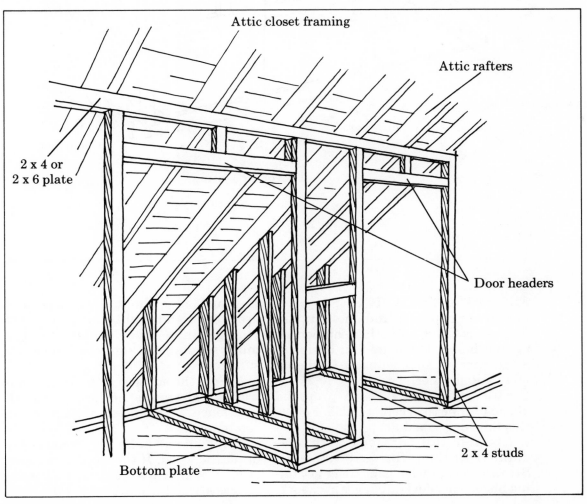

Attic closet framing

Attic rafters

2 x 4 or
2 x 6 plate

Door headers

2 x 4 studs

Bottom plate

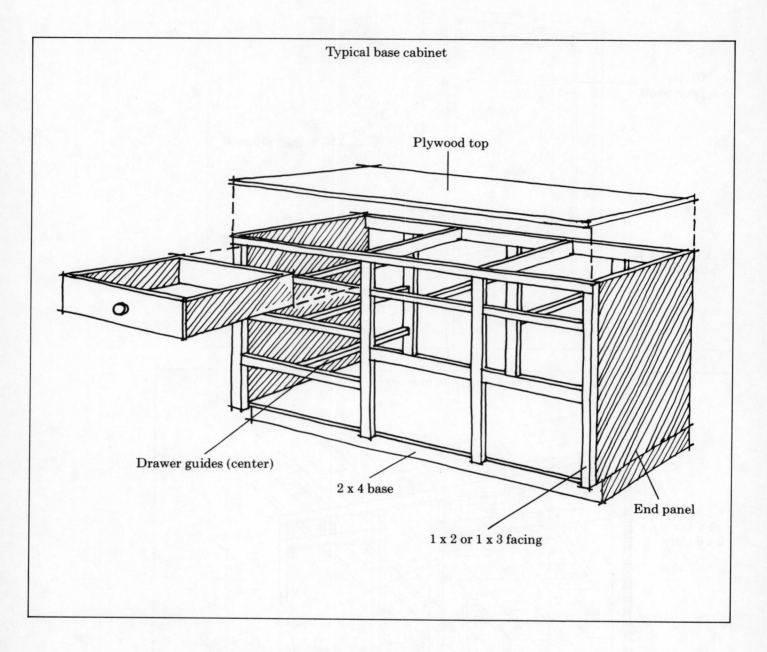

Typical base cabinet

Plywood top

Drawer guides (center)

2 x 4 base

1 x 2 or 1 x 3 facing

End panel

FINISHING TECHNIQUES

Storage cabinets and shelving are finished just like any other component in your home. There are four basic finishes: varnish, shellac, paint (and enamel), and lacquer.

All surfaces have to be prepared ahead of time to accept a finish. Follow this finishing schedule:

1. Sand the surfaces with medium-grit, then fine-grit abrasive. Stretch the abrasive paper over a sanding block; the block produces a smooth, flat surface without dips, digs, and grooves. Sand lightly. Since most storage units involve plywood, too much sanding can ruin the top veneer surface.

2. Seal the surface with clear, penetrating sealer or shellac. If the wood will be stained, you can use a stain/sealer combination.

3. Fill all nail holes with wood putty or plastic wood. If the wood is an open grained one, such as oak, you may want to use a wood filler. Check with your

paint dealer before you use a wood filler, however; fillers can make the surface of the wood look horrible and can reduce the quality of finishes used over them. Finish over fillers tends to chip and flake.

Have plenty of ventilation

When working with any finishing materials, make sure the room is ventilated and that it is as dust free as possible. You may accomplish this by not sweeping the floor before you start the finishing process and by closing heating/air-conditioning vents. Use a window exhaust fan, or simply open a window.

There are many new finishes on the market today. The ones we describe below are the basic ones. But before you apply any finish, be sure to read the manufacturer's instructions on the container; you may find slight variations.

Varnish finish

We recommend a synthetic resin varnish or a polyurethane varnish because the finish dries fast. You can buy other types, which include phenolic and alkyd. Spar varnish is used for exterior finishes and should be used on outdoor storage pieces.

Apply the varnish using a 2-inch wide brush. Go across the surface of the material in long narrow strips; then cross these strips and fill in the missed spots.

Instead you may wish to thin the varnish with several drops of turpentine; then brush on the varnish as you

Selecting abrasive paper

Aluminum oxide Silicon carbide Garnet	Emery	Flint
Very fine	600 500 400 (10/0) 360 320 (9/0) 280 (8/0) 240 (7/0) 220 (6/0)		Very fine
Fine	180 (5/0) 3/0 150 (4/0) 2/0 120 (3/0) 1/0		Fine
Medium	100 (2/0) ½ 80 (1/0) 1 60 (½) 1½		Medium
Coarse	50 (1) 2 40 (1½) 2½ 36 (2) 3		Coarse
Very coarse	30 (2½) 24 (3) 20 (3½) 16 (4) 12 (4½)		Very coarse

would paint. Work the varnish into a thin coating on the surface of the wood, and tip this off with the end of the brush in the direction of the grain.

You will need two to three coats of varnish for the perfect finish. Lightly buff the dry finish between coats with 0000 (grade) steel wool. After the final coat dries, wax the surface.

Shellac finish

Shellac has the reputation of being difficult to use. It isn't. But you do have to use a lot of elbow grease when applying it.

First, wipe the surface of the wood with a tack rag. (You should always wipe the surface of any finishing project with a tack rag—regardless of the finish.)

Stir the shellac before you apply it. Don't shake shellac; this causes bubbles in the liquid, which are difficult to work out.

Buy a new paint brush, and apply 1-pound cut shellac to the surface. Flow the shellac on the surface with long, even brush strokes and lap the strokes so the material is evenly applied.

- Let the shellac dry for two hours.
- Lightly rub the wood with 0000 steel wool.
- Go over the surface with a tack rag.
- Apply the second coat of shellac, and let it dry for 3 hours.
- Lightly rub the surface with 0000 steel wool.
- Use the tack rag again.
- Apply a third coat of shellac, and let it dry for 24 hours.
- Rub down the finish with 0000 steel wool.
- Wax the surface with paste wax, and buff the wax to a gloss.
- Give the surface another coat of paste wax, and buff it again.

Lacquer finish

Lacquer may be applied with a brush or with a spray can; we recommend a spray can because it makes the application easier.

When using lacquer, work fast. If you brush it on, thin it slightly with lacquer thinner; lacquer should not be used when it becomes stiff.

Whether you brush or spray, work in small areas. Otherwise, the lacquer will dry before you can catch up with the wet edges.

- After the first coat, wait 4 hours for the lacquer to harden.
- Buff the surface lightly with 0000 steel wool.
- Apply a second coat of lacquer.
- Buff the surface when dry with 0000 steel wool; wax and buff.

Paint and enamel finishes

You can apply paint or enamel with a brush or spray can. If you choose the spray method, follow the manufacturer's instructions on the container. Follow these steps if you brush on paint or enamel:

1. Thin the liquid slightly.

2. Work with a 2-inch brush. Either float the finish over the surface or brush it into the surface—just like varnish. (Enamel is varnish with color added.)

3. After the first coat dries—in 24 to 36 hours—rub the surface lightly with 0000 steel wool. Clean the surface with a tack rag.

4. Give the surface two more coats of paint or enamel, rubbing with steel wool and cleaning with a tack rag between coats. Wax.

Finishing fir plywood

Douglas fir plywood panels have a wild grain. The panels are easy to paint, as described above, but are difficult to stain. If you use enamel over fir plywood panels, be sure you seal the surface first with penetrating sealer. To use stain follow these 4 steps:

1. Apply two coats of orange shellac thinned with equal parts of denatured alcohol.

2. When the shellac is dry, lightly sand the surface.

3. Apply the stain.

4. When the stain dries, cover it with clear lacquer.

Basic Storage Assembly Techniques

After you decide on a storage design, put the design down on paper—we suggest using graph paper. This way, you can anticipate the materials needed, special dimensions, and building details.

We also suggest that you spend some time shopping in a home center store with your attention especially focused on base and wall cabinets, unfinished furniture, and hardware. You will be amazed at the different storage items you will find; the shopping tour is bound to spark an idea or two.

In this chapter you will find a collection of tips on assembly techniques. The tips are classified as to sawing, setting hinges, making wood joints, and applying hardware. There are some tool-use suggestions, also, to make the job go easier for you.

WOOD JOINTS

With hand tools there are three wood joints you can cut and assemble:

1. Butt joints
2. Miters
3. Laps (cross, middle, half)

Although they are more difficult, you may be able to make two others:

1. A rabbet joint
2. A dado joint

Fancy joints such as a stopped dado, dovetail, half-blind, blind miter, squared splice, and through single are *extremely* difficult to make without power tool equipment. Fortunately, the three basic hand-tool joints are typical of most storage units. Miters and laps take careful planning and cutting. Don't hurry.

See the Index to find information on how to cut and assemble butt joints, miters, and laps. We do not show how to cut the fancy joints; when you have progressed that far in cabinetmaking, you won't need our instruction.

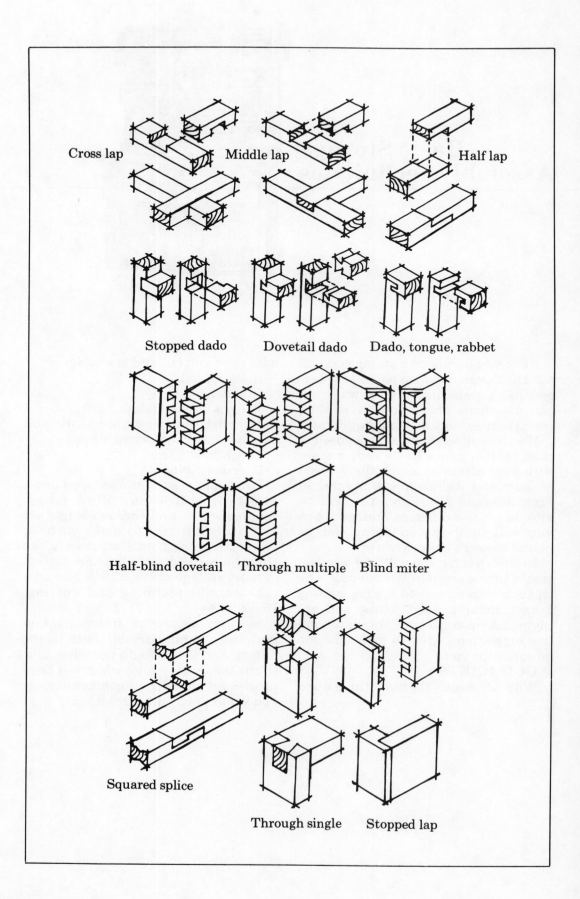

Cross lap Middle lap Half lap

Stopped dado Dovetail dado Dado, tongue, rabbet

Half-blind dovetail Through multiple Blind miter

Squared splice

Through single Stopped lap

MAKING BASIC WOOD JOINTS

Typical butt joint. The edges or faces of the boards or lumber are fastened together flush with nails or screws and glue; screws have more holding power and are better than nails. If you join a series of boards or lumber edge-to-edge, you must support these joints with wood or metal cleats.

Miter joint. The edges of the boards or lumber are fastened together at a 45-degree angle, which is cut in a miter box or with a power saw. Like a butt joint, miter joints may be fastened with nails or screws and glue. Since miter joints tend to be weak, you may strengthen them with metal angles. (See metal angles in Index.)

Miter box and backsaw are used to cut boards and lumber square and at an angle. To cut a 45-degree angle, the backsaw is inserted in the angled slots, as shown; hold the board tightly against the back of the miter box so it doesn't slip. Any sawing error will be compounded when you assemble the different wooden components.

Always check miter cuts with a combination square. If the cut is slightly off, you may be able to square it with a block plane or medium-grit sandpaper stretched over a sanding block. Use a light touch with the plane or sandpaper; both cut quickly. Check the cut with the square often.

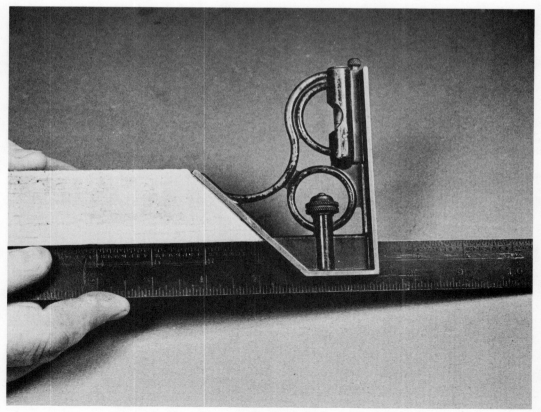

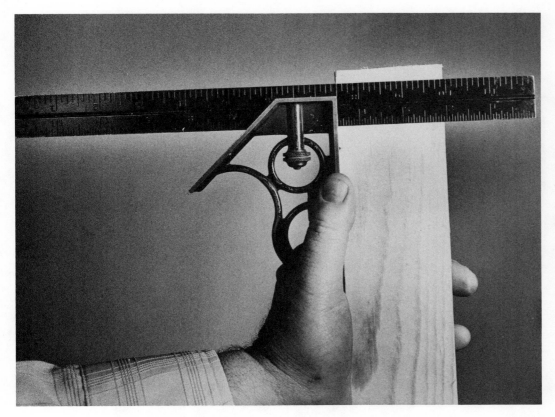

Square ends are a must in any carpentry project. Use a miter box to make this cut, or, if the material doesn't fit the miter box, use a combination saw. For panel materials, use a large framing or combination square. To guide the saw, you can clamp a board along the cutoff line; check often, however, to make sure the saw is square with the cutoff line.

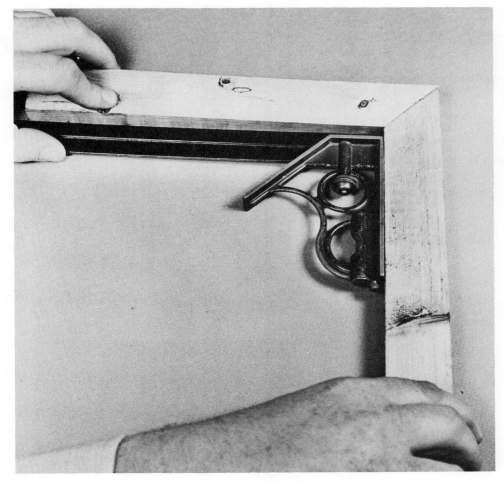

When assembling mitered material, use a combination square, as shown, to align the materials properly. Screws and glue are the best fasteners for almost any wood joint. If screws are too large for the material, use finishing nails and glue. Miter joints are usually specified in cabinet facing and trim. To assure a better fit, test the miter on the cabinet before you assemble the miter joint.

End joints and edge joints must be reinforced with wooden cleats or metal reinforcing plates; they are extremely weak and should be used only when little weight or stress will be applied to the joints—as for facing or trim. You can get more strength into these joints by mortising the metal plate into the wood.

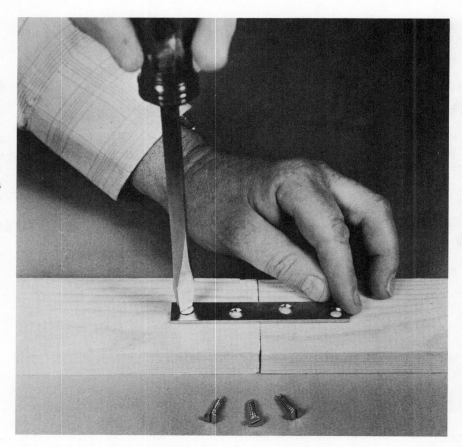

Butt-jointed corners should be screwed (or nailed) and glued, then reinforced with a metal angle. This strengthens the joint so that it can be used in basic framing or facing and trim. Make sure the cuts are square; joints that don't fit together well are weak.

Dividers or stretchers in framing members are reinforced with T-shaped metal plates. This butt joint should also be screwed (or nailed) and glued together. Since this joint is fairly strong, you may use the divider as support for light drawer hardware in a cabinet installation. When nailing panel material to the framing, have a helper hold the framing while you hammer in the fasteners. Support on the backside will help prevent the joints from loosening.

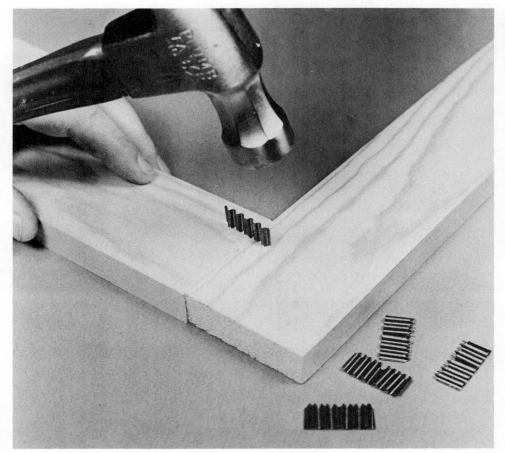

Wiggle nails, or corrugated fasteners, may be used to assemble butt joints in *very light framing.* Nail and glue the joint to give it more reinforcement. Tap the wiggle nails as easily as possible into the wood; if you pound on one edge, the fastener tends to work up and out of the wood on the other edge. Use two or three wiggle nails per joint; space the nails evenly. Wiggle nails may be countersunk.

CONSTRUCTING A SIMPLE DADO JOINT

Scotch fasteners are a variation of wiggle nails which offer about the same support to butt joints and are easier to drive. Use nails and glue to support the joint. Unlike wiggle nails, scotch fasteners are very difficult to countersink; use them where you don't care if they show.

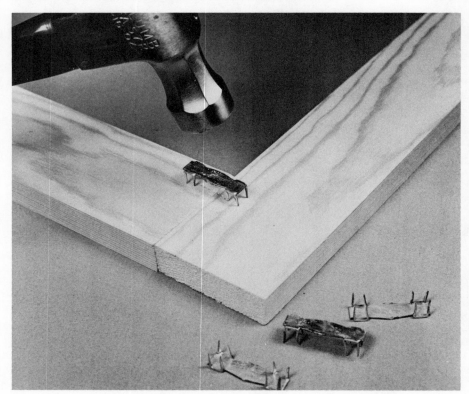

For most storage and cabinet framing, use this simple dado joint. It is very easy to cut with a backsaw or combination saw and can be assembled with nails, screws, and glue. Lay out the joint, as shown, using the joining member as a template or guide. After you mark the cutout lines, check them with a square; the pieces must fit together tightly for a strong joint.

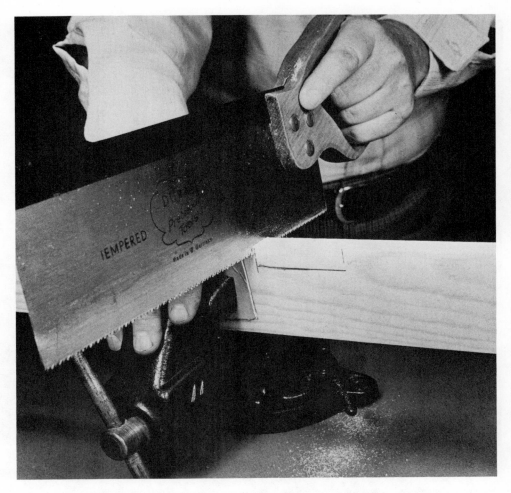

Cut the dado with a backsaw or crosscut saw. Saw slightly outside the marked lines, keeping the saw square with the wood at all times. Check this with your combination square. Also, make sure you do not saw deeper than you want the dado to be.

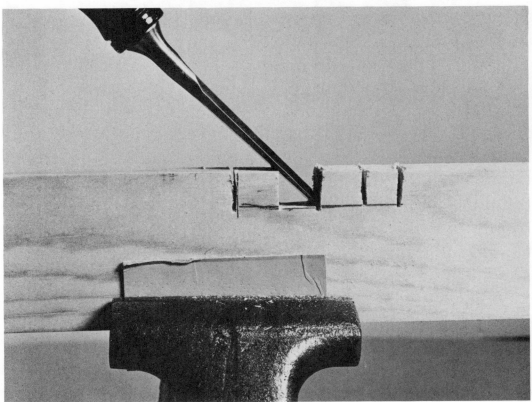

After you make the end cuts, make a series of saw cuts between the end cuts. Go to the exact depth of the cut with each saw kerf. You need only several saw cuts in this space; don't overdo it, or you may damage the joint.

With a sharp wide chisel, remove the excess wood from the dado. The little pieces of wood will flip right out without much leverage from the chisel. Smooth the bottom of the cut slightly, and check the joint for fit. If the fit is too tight, chisel out the excess. Test as you cut, however.

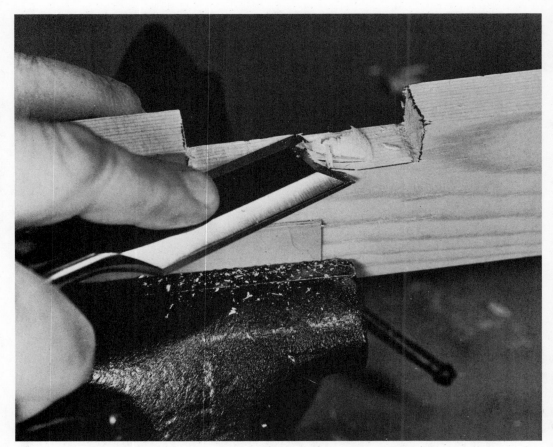

Assemble the dado joint with nails, screws, and glue. The depth of the joint should be the thickness of the joining wood member. This is called a flush joint. If you want a recessed joint, you can make the dado cut slightly deeper, or you can create a raised joint by making the dado cut shallower.

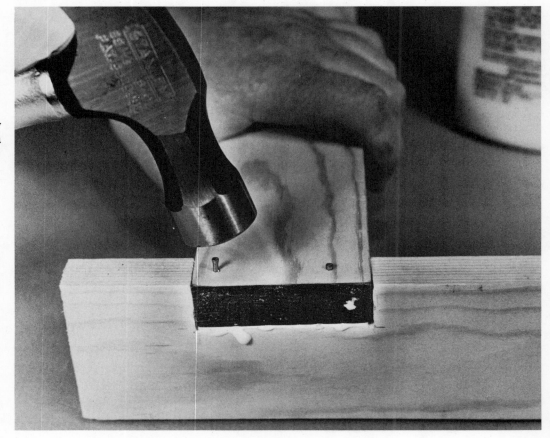

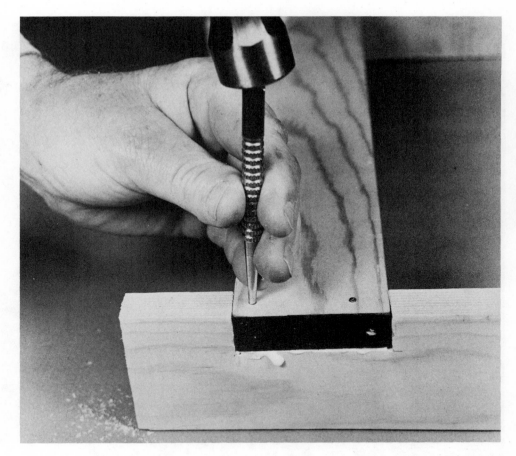

Countersink the nailheads with a nail set. If you use screws, drill pilot holes for the screws, and countersink the screws flush with the wood. If you use a hardwood for the framing, such as oak, you should drill tiny pilot holes for the nails to prevent the wood from splitting.

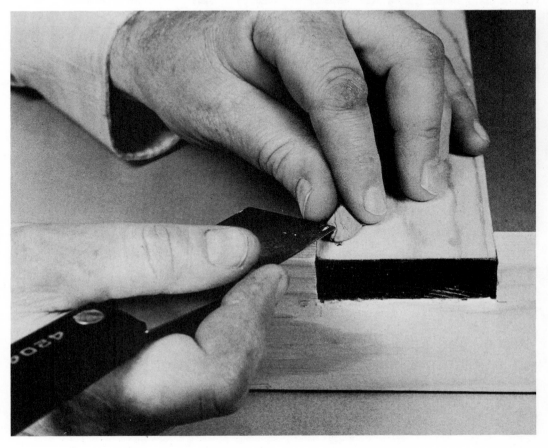

If the nail holes will show, fill the holes with plastic wood or water putty. Leave both fillers slightly high in the holes because the filler tends to shrink when it dries; then lightly sand the wood and filler, and remove any excess glue. The wood is now ready to seal and finish.

A *half lap joint* is almost as easy to make with hand tools as a dado joint. This joint is good to use for decorative facings and, because it is strong, for basic framing (drawer frames and slides). Outline the cut with a pencil and use a combination saw or backsaw. The depth of the cut depends on the project: the joint may be flush, slightly raised, or slightly recessed. To hide the screw fasteners, countersink the screws into the wood, and fill the holes with plastic wood or water putty, or counterbore the holes and fill the holes with dowel plugs, as shown. A piece of tape wrapped around the drill bit at the depth you want the counterbored hole to be will act as a gauge.

Insert the dowel plugs (buy them at home center stores) in the counterbored hole with glue; push them in firmly, and wipe away any excess glue. Dowel plugs usually have a convex top; if your project calls for a flush-pegged look, simply cut the dowel plugs from the dowel rod. Since dowels usually are birch, you may get a slightly different finish from the trim stock you are using. If this is a problem, experiment with the finish on a scrap piece of dowel until you get the finish you want.

FASTENING FRAMING TO WALLS, FLOORS, DOORS

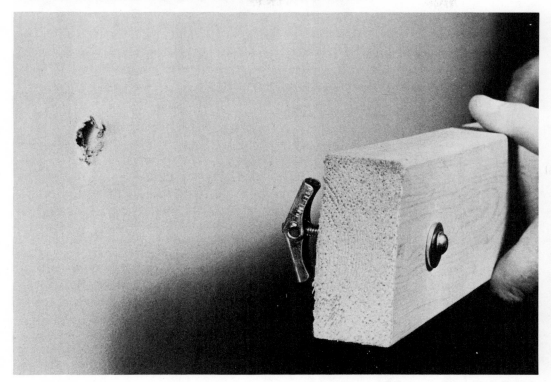

Toggle bolts are used to fasten framing and furring strips to gypsum wallboard. Toggle bolts have spring-activated flanges that flip open on the backside of the wall. When the bolt is tightened, the flanges grip the back of the wall, holding the framing member in position. To use toggle bolts, drill holes in the wall where the bolts will be inserted; then drill holes through the framing member to match the holes in the wall. Both sets of holes should be in perfect alignment, so be careful when you lay out the job. Insert the toggle bolts through the framing and screw on the flanges; stick the bolt and flange through the holes in the wall; tighten the bolts with a screwdriver.

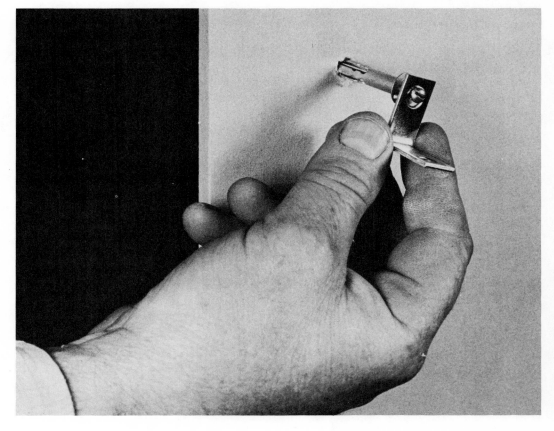

Molly bolts also are used to fasten framing and furring to gypsum wallboard. To use these fasteners, drill the desired number of holes in the wall; insert the base of the plugs into the holes, and remove the screws. Run the screws through the framing, and drive them into the base.

Behind the wall, the Molly bolts flange out, as shown. By tightening the screws in the bases, you activate the flanges, which grip the back of the wall and hold the framing tight against the front of the wall. As in working with toggle bolts, be sure you are accurate in job layout; framing and furring members must be horizontally level or plumb (vertically level.)

Hollow-core door fasteners are the smaller cousins of Molly bolts. Use them to anchor framing and brackets to the backs of hollow core doors, which usually are skinned with a thin piece of wood veneer. The fasteners are used the very same way as Molly bolts: drill a hole— or a series of holes—in the door; insert the fastener; remove the screw; insert the screw in the framing member or hanger; activate the screw in the base.

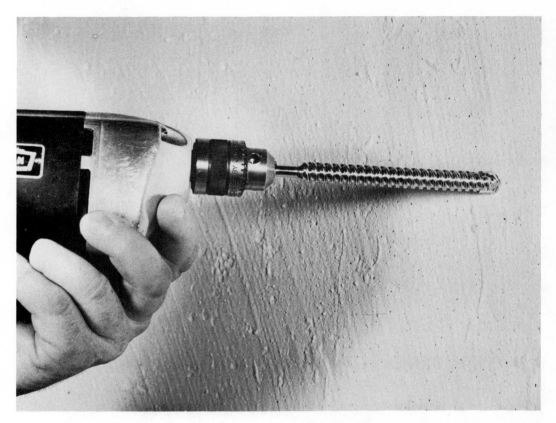

Anchoring framing to concrete or brick walls requires either holes for lead expansion anchors or fiber plugs for light framing. A masonry drill in a portable electric drill is the fast way to make the holes, which should be equal in depth to the length of the anchors.

If you don't have a power drill, you can punch holes for anchors and plugs in concrete or brick with a star drill. Twist the star drill in the hole as you strike it with a sledge hammer; tiny flutes on the end of the drill will auger out powdered concrete.

Sill plates and nailers (usually 2 by 4s) may be fastened to concrete floors with lead anchors and lag bolts. Drill holes for the lead anchors with a masonry bit in a power drill or a star drill. If the floor is wooden, use common nails to secure these framing members; if the floor is carpeted, remove the carpeting; if the floor is uneven, use cedar shingles to shim the framing level. The shingles are tapered. Shingles also can be used to level or plumb framing members fastened to walls and ceilings.

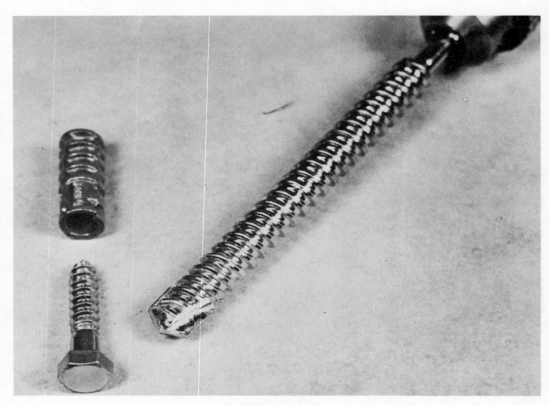

Concrete nails may be used to fasten framing and furring to concrete and concrete block surfaces. The nails are very tough; you should drill pilot holes for the nails in the framing or furring before you drive the nails into the concrete. Hit these nails squarely and evenly; otherwise, you may chip the concrete as the nails go into it.

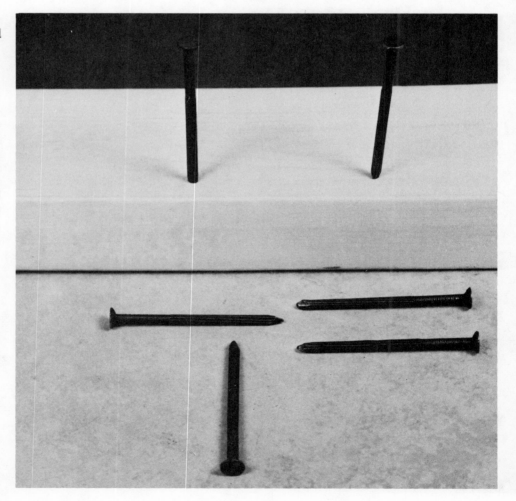

USING LEVELING AND SPECIAL MARKING TOOLS

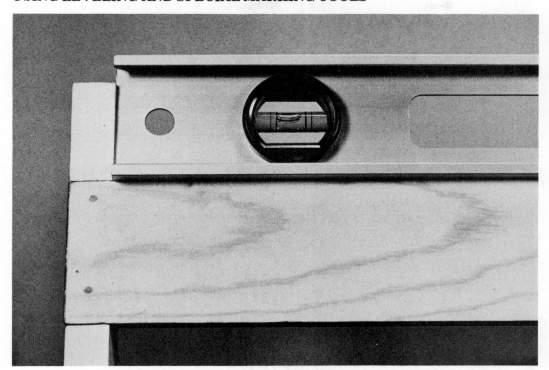

All framing must be horizontally level, regardless of the storage project. Use a spirit level to check levelness. When the bubble in the level glass is between the two marked lines, the framing is level.

Plumb is vertically level. When the bubble in the spirit level is centered between the two marked lines, the framing is plumb, or vertically level. Always double-check for level and plumb. A slight variation can compound the error so the work looks sloppy when you are finished with the project.

A plumb bob is used to mark plumb, or vertical level. The bob is a weight with a pointed end fastened to a piece of chalk line. The line is tied to a nail at the top of the work and when the plumb bob stops swinging on the line, you have established vertical level. At this point, hold the plumb bob firmly and snap the chalk line (which should be coated with a blue chalk material). The line is tranferred to the wall surface. Always double check the line with a square or level. You can use a chalk line (without plumb bob) to establish horizontal level over large surfaces such as walls, ceilings, and floors. Stretch the line between two nails; make sure the line is square. Then snap the line on the flat surface.

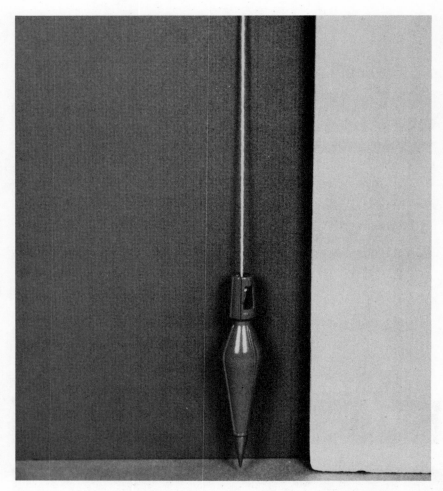

Duplicating odd shapes, such as the area around baseboards, is done with dividers or a compass. Set the framing member against the trim, as shown, then, open the dividers or compass about the width of the thickness of the trim. Let one leg of the compass or dividers follow the contour of the trim, while the other leg scribes the same contour on the framing or trim piece.

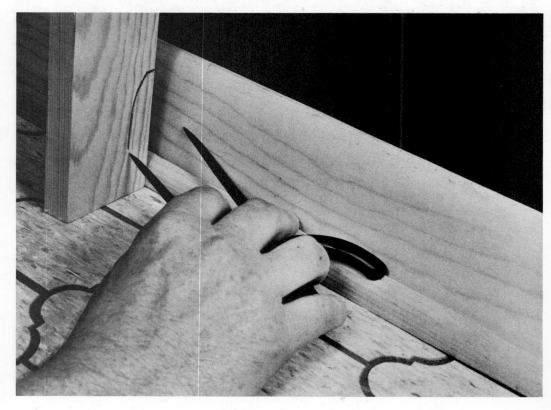

Use a marking gauge to scribe cutting lines (with the grain of the wood) on boards and lumber that have a squared edge. Marking gauges have a ruled scale that provides a guide for the depth of the cut. When you use a marking gauge, make sure you press it firmly against the edge of the material. Keep this pressure firm and even throughout the marking process; otherwise, the line may not be true.

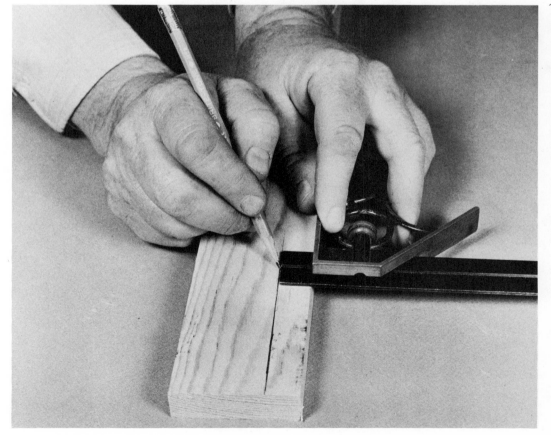

If you don't have a marking gauge, substitute a combination square for the marking job. Hold the square tightly against the squared edge and move the blade of the square and marking pencil at the same time. A combination square also may be used as a depth gauge when making mortise and dado cuts in wood. You simply set the blade at the right depth, and lock it in place with the thumbscrew on the base of the square.

USING SMOOTHING TOOLS AND SPECIAL SAWS

A jack plane may be used to smooth saw cuts on framing and trim members. Apply the pressure forward on the plane as you first push it into the wood. Then apply the pressure to both ends of the plane at the middle of the stroke and to the handle at the end of the stroke. The plane has a shaving action similar to that of a chisel. Go easily; you don't need to power a plane. Take little bites with the blade, and check the work often to make sure it is square.

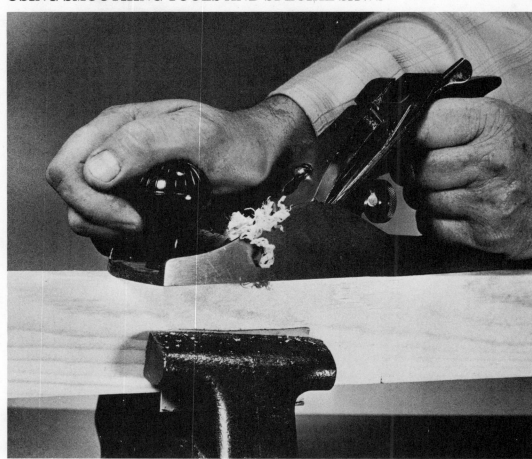

A block plane is used to smooth end-grain and other delicate planing jobs. Apply the pressure at the front of the plane with your index finger. Additional pressure should be from the palm of your hand over the blade housing. Both jack and block plane blades may be set for depth with a thumbscrew. A lever on the back of the blade housing adjusts the angle of the blade in the slot in the plane bed. Before using either plane, check for depth of cut on a piece of scrap wood.

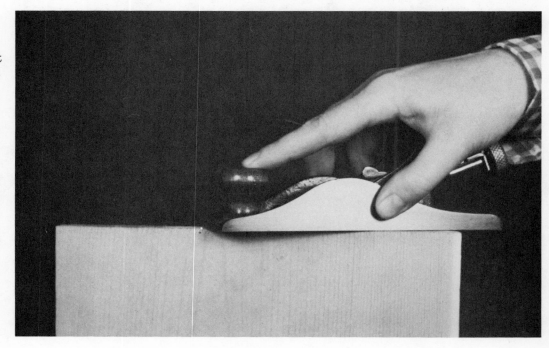

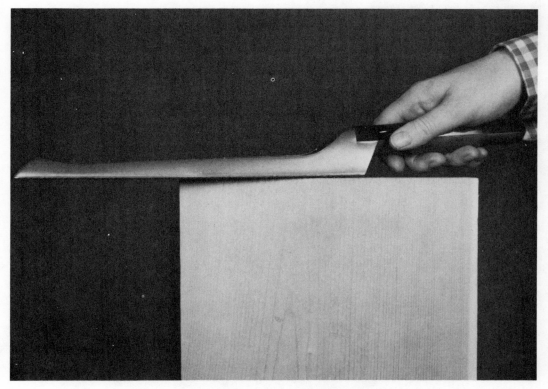

Multibladed forming plane (Surform) is best for smoothing end-grain and other planing jobs. You can buy many different types of blades, which are interchangeable—blades for plastic, metal, and other materials. You can use this plane across the grain, with the grain, or against the grain. The tool also serves as a rasp, file, and coarse sandpaper.

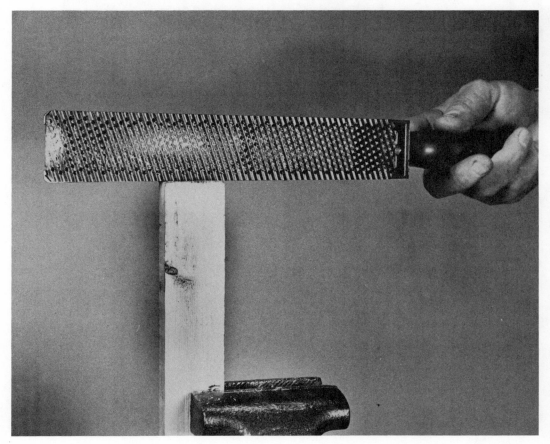

Bottom of multibladed plane looks like this: a series of very sharp cutting edges. The tool is fairly inexpensive, and the blades are easy to interchange by simply removing screws.

Holes in panels and boards can be cut to accept components, such as electrical junction boxes, with a portable electric sabre saw. Use a combination blade, and saw from the finished side of the panel. You also can use a sabre saw for cutting large round holes with diameters too large for regular drill and expansion bits.

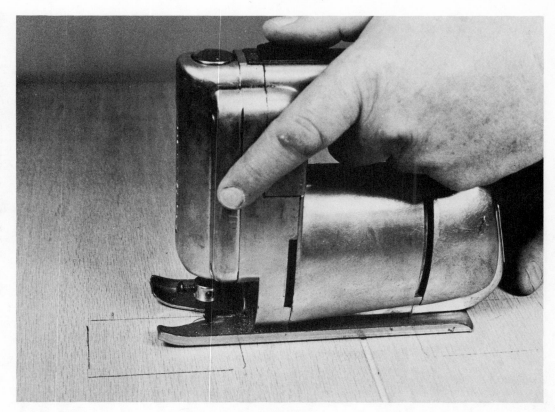

If you don't have a sabre saw, use a keyhole saw to cut holes in panels and boards. First drill a hole into the material to accept the tip of the keyhole saw. Drill from the finished side of the panel or board, and back the material with a piece of scrap lumber so the drill bit doesn't split or dig the panel as it cuts through.

Connect the holes with the keyhole saw, cutting on the scribed lines. Some keyhole saws have interchangeable blades. We recommend that you buy the type with a rip blade, combination blade, and metal-cutting blade. For most cuts in panels, as shown, use a combination blade. This blade will provide a smoother cut—especially on prefinished paneling.

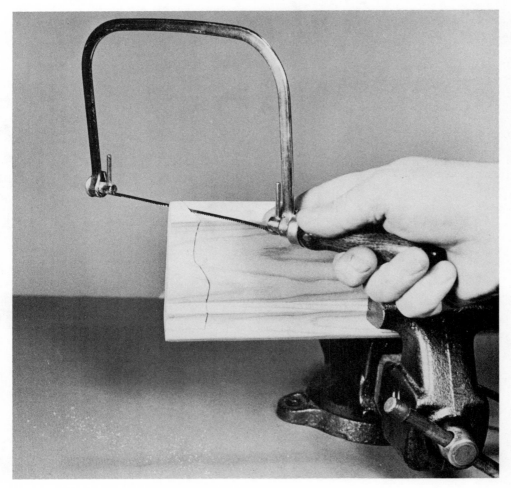

For angled cuts in molding and trim, use a coping saw. This saw has a blade which may be turned to match the angles you want to cut. You turn the blade by moving the little metal pins at each end of the blade. Coping saw blades also are interchangeable. The more teeth to the blade, the smoother the cut.

CUTTING MORTISES FOR HINGES AND LOCKS

Outline the shape of the hinge on the edge of the door with a pencil. Be especially accurate with the marks; the hinge must fit properly to work satisfactorily. Double-check these lines with a combination square or framing square. If the lines don't match, try again until they match perfectly with the hinge outline.

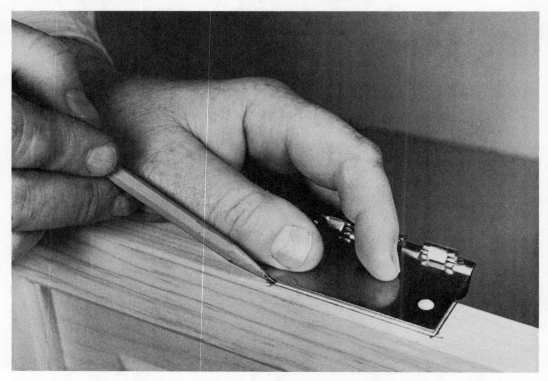

With a sharp wide chisel, cut in the hinge outline. Keep the flat part of the chisel (the back) against the penciled lines. Also, make sure the depth of the chisel cut is the exact thickness of the hinge. If you make a mistake here, you can shim up the hinge with a piece of cardboard.

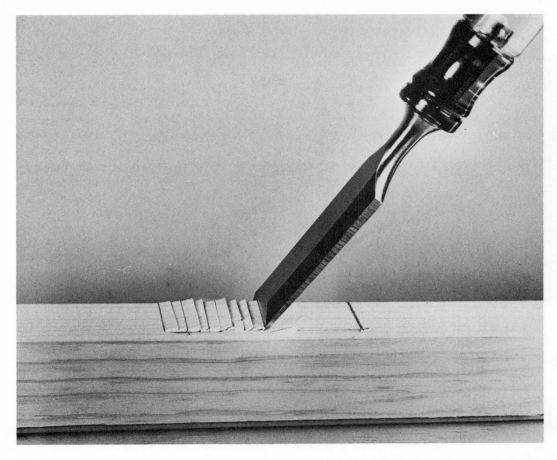

Make a series of shallow chisel cuts within the lines. Tap the chisel into the wood at a slight angle, using a wooden mallet or rubber hammer. Do not use a metal hammer, or you may damage the chisel handle. Also, don't use the palm of your hand to drive the chisel. Your hand is not as accurate as a mallet or rubber hammer.

Clean out the mortise with the chisel. Keep the tapered edge of the chisel down, and tap the chisel lightly with a mallet or rubber hammer. Go easily; sharp chisels cut fast. When these chips have been removed, smooth the cut with the chisel, tapered side up. Test the hinge in the mortise. If the mortise is not deep enough, remove the excess wood with planing-like cuts. Do not attempt to make another series of shallow chisel cuts.

Invisible hinges (Soss) are expensive, but they produce a smoothly operating door. The hinges are packaged with a template pattern, which you use to locate the holes for the drill. Use a bradawl or sharp nail for locating these drill guide holes.

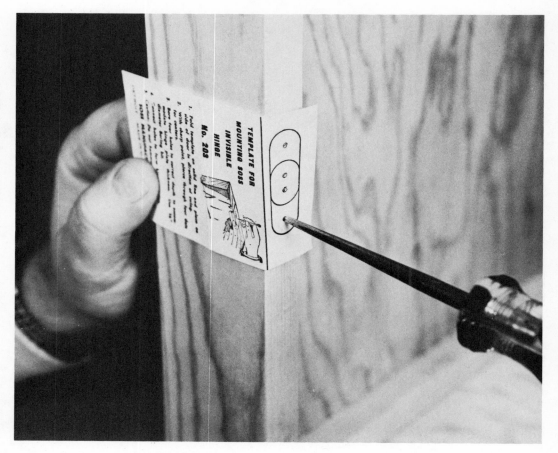

Drill the outside holes first, since they are not as deep as the other holes. You can test the depth of the cut by inserting part of the hinge into the hole. The cuts have to be accurate; a piece of tape on the drill serves as a depth gauge.

Clean out the drilled holes with a narrow chisel, and connect the cuts by removing the excess wood with a chisel. Work slowly, removing small shavings of wood one at a time. Test the hinge in the opening from time to time to make sure the fit is accurate.

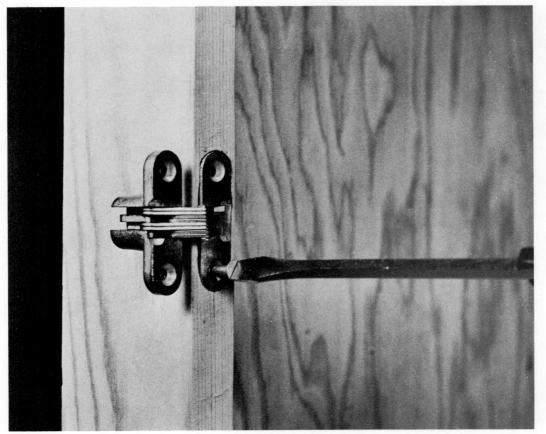

Screw the hinge into position. If the fit is accurate, remove the screws and hinge. Align the template on the edge of the door, and repeat the process. Most door schedules call for two invisible hinges; this means you will have four sets of mortises to make. When all cuts meet your requirements, insert the hinges into the holes, and screw them into place.

Deep mortises and pocket mortises are made with a drill and chisel. Mark the mortise on the edge of the door or framing, and drill out the wood to the depth you want. The edge of the drill bit should match the line at both ends; the drill bit should be exactly as wide as you want the mortise to be. Draw a center line, between the outside lines, as a guide for the drill bit, as shown.

Connect the holes with a sharp, wide chisel. Make sure the chisel is square to the wood so the cuts will be square within the mortise. Keep the tapered edge of the chisel inside the cuts, and tap the chisel with a wooden mallet or rubber hammer. Put the hinge or lock into the mortise as you clean it out. The fit should be as tight as possible. The depth isn't too critical; you always can shim up the hardware with a piece of cardboard.

USING SCREWS AND NAILS

The screwdriver blade must fit the screw slot. If the blade is narrower than the slot, the screwdriver may damage it when pressure is applied to drive or draw the screw. If the blade is wider than the screw slot, the blade may mar the wood surrounding the head of the screw. Always use the longest screwdriver you have; the length provides more driving and drawing power.

Special countersinking bits are used in a portable electric drill. The bits drill pilot holes for the screws, as well as countersink the holes for the screwheads. The bits are made in a wide range of sizes. Pilot holes for screws should always be the same size as the threaded part of the screw.

Countersink bits for hand drills also are available. Drill the pilot hole for the screw first. Make the diameter the same as the threaded part of the screw; then use the countersink bit to countersink the pilot hole. When you think the hole is deep enough for the screwhead, test the screw in the hole. The screwhead should be flush with the surrounding wood surface.

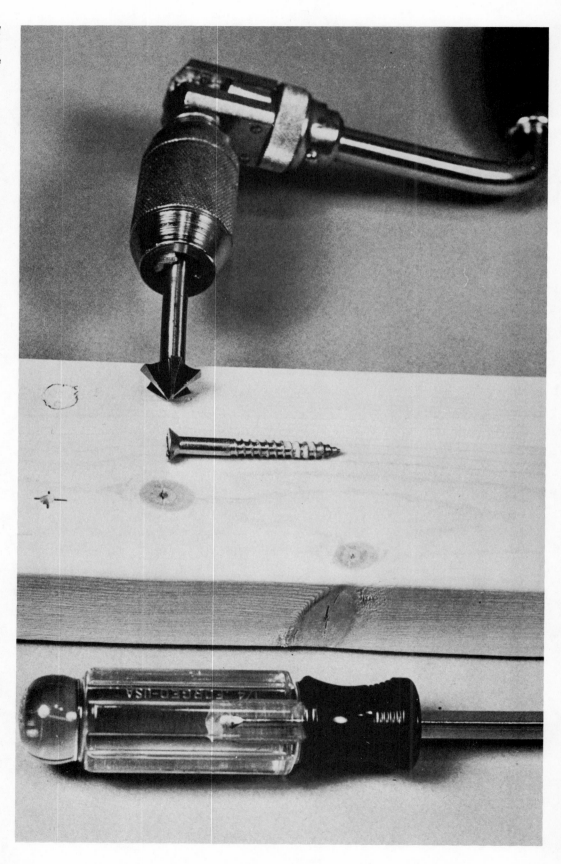

Nails often need pilot holes to prevent the wood from splitting when the nail is driven home. You may use a bradawl to punch a pilot hole for nails, or use a tiny drill bit, slightly smaller than the shank of the nail. A bradawl, shown, is especially useful when you have a lot of brads or small nails to drive.

Cabinet and Drawer Building Techniques

Square wood cleats help reinforce butt joints and cabinet corners. The cleats also provide fastening members for cabinet backs. Assemble the joint first with nails or screws and glue; then nail and glue on the cleat, as shown. Nail from both directions—down through the top and through the side. The cleats should be as tight as possible against the panels.

To support cabinet backs, use a length of quarter-round molding nailed and glued to the cabinet panels, as shown, or use square wooden cleats. The molding should be recessed into the cabinet the thickness of the cabinet back. The molding joints around the cabinet do not have to be butted tightly together, since the cabinet back will hide them.

The cabinet back fits against the molding pieces, thus providing a recessed or flush back and creating a neater appearance by covering the edges of the panels. You may use hardboard or plywood for cabinet backs; we recommend hardboard. If you do use hardboard, drill pilot holes for the nails. Hardboard is extremely dense; too much pounding may damage the molding.

Shelf supports may be simple cleats, like these, or you may use quarter-round molding for supports. Either way, nail and glue the supports to the sides of the cabinet. The shelves simply ride on the cleats. Do not nail the shelves to the cleats; the shelves must have room for expansion or contraction.

Reinforce joints inside the cabinet with metal angle brackets screwed to the panels, as shown. You also may use triangular glue blocks for reinforcement; cut the blocks diagonally from 2 by 2s to form the triangle. When working with panels over framing, simply nail the panels to the framing member; you don't need extra reinforcement.

Dividers within a cabinet may be fabricated with small pieces of quarter round or trim, which, in parallel, form a groove; the divider slides between these pieces. If you have a power saw, you can cut dadoes for the dividers. You may not need special dado blades for this. A couple of passes through the saw can cut the dado wide enough to accept the dividers, which are usually ⅛ to ¼ inch thick.

Case and cabinet pieces usually are trimmed with a framework of 1 by 2s or 1 by 3s. The trim may be prefabricated and nailed to the piece; or you can trim the piece one stick at a time. The trim pieces can be mitered at the corners, or the pieces can be butt-jointed. (See framing techniques in Index.) Use finishing nails to attach the trim to the cabinet; countersink the nails, and fill the holes with wood filler or water putty.

Raw plywood edges on hardboard-faced plywood panels may be trimmed with veneer tape. The tape is real wood veneer and is applied with contact cement. You can buy veneer tape in different widths and in different wood veneers to match the panels you are using.

Standard moldings—screen molding, flat molding, half-round molding—also may be used to hide raw plywood edges. Use glue and nails to attach the moldings; countersink the nailheads, and fill the holes with plastic wood or water putty.

Sliding door track can be covered with a trim piece of wood, as shown; or you can hide just the edge of the panel with veneer tape or standard moldings. As a rule, both edges and track are covered for design purposes. Use glue when you fasten on the trim pieces to provide a stronger joint.

Drawers

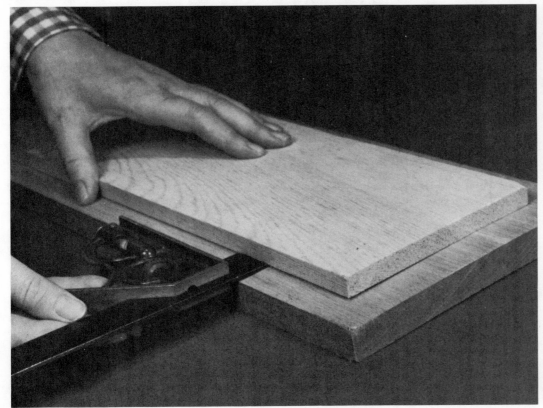

Power equipment is not required to make simple design drawers. Center a piece of ½-inch thick material on the back of the drawer, as shown here. Buy good material; the drawer back and front should be free of any warp. Nail and glue the back to the drawer back. Weight both pieces until the glue dries, if you don't have clamps to hold the pieces tight.

Nail and glue the sides of the drawer (also ½-inch thick) material to the drawer back. These joints are butt joints; they should be reinforced with small metal angle brackets at each corner. Wipe away excess glue, and let the glue dry before you add the metal angles.

The hardboard drawer bottom floats on cleats made of quarter-round or other small standard moldings. You may want to attach these moldings to the drawer sides, back, and end before you assemble the components. Use glue and tiny brads to attach the support pieces.

Drawer guide is a piece of 1 by 2 that is fastened to the drawer framework in the cabinet. The framework goes together in simple butt joints and is fastened with wiggle nails or glue and nails. The guide is centered in this framework and also is fastened to the framework with wiggle nails. You can reinforce the joints with metal plates. Cut a dado in the back of the drawer to match the drawer guide, as shown.

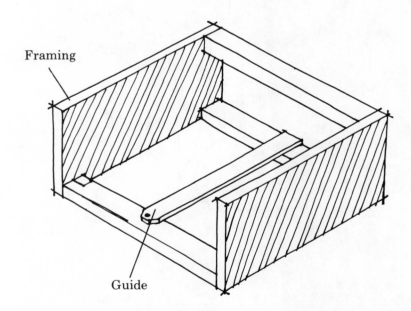

Framing

Guide

Special Hardware for Storage Shelves and Cabinets

Standard cabinet and storage hardware includes continuous (piano) hinges, at the top; semi-concealed hinges, upper left; pair of off-set hinges, upper and lower right; butt hinges, lower left; and invisible hinges, center. There is also a variety of sliding door tracks, aluminum door tracks, sliding tray hardware, support hardware, cup hooks, and many others. We recommend that you spend a couple of hours shopping in a home center or hardware store to familiarize yourself with what is available.

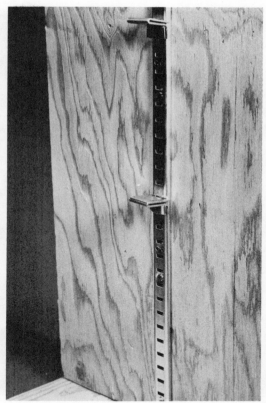

Far left:
Adjustable shelf brackets are metal, and you mount them on the sides of cabinets or walls to hang shelves. Installation is no mystery. Screw the brackets to the cabinet or wall, as shown, and punch in a pilot hole for the mounting screws with a bradawl or drill bit. You can buy brackets with a low or high profile, depending on your cabinet or shelving design.

Left:
Small, tablike brackets also are adjustable. This hardware generally is used inside cabinets, rather than for heavier wall shelving. The brackets are mounted with screws to the sides of the case pieces and can be painted to match the cabinet interior. The tabs allow space between shelves to be adjusted. If glass shelving is used, glue pieces of felt on the top of the bracket inserts for padding.

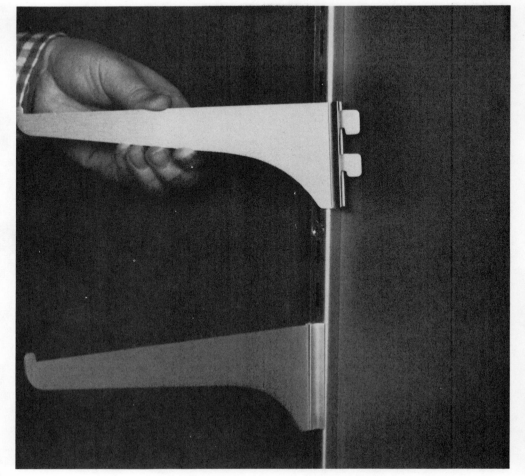

The shelf brackets fit into notches in the side brackets. Make sure the shelf supports are securely in the slots; if the support brackets are not slotted properly, the shelving may tip. Shelf brackets mounted on a wall should be fastened to the studs, if possible. Otherwise, use Molly bolts or toggle bolts to mount the brackets properly.

Aluminum sliding door track simply screws onto the cabinet panels or framing; you don't have to cut dadoes for the doors. You can buy aluminum fixtures and moldings for inside corners, outside corners, and you can buy trim for paneled storage cabinets and shelving.

Doors that support heavy weight should be hinged with continuous (piano) hinges. These hinges are installed directly over the edges of the door and framing, or the hinges may be mortised. If the door is a heavy one, such as an exterior door put into service as an interior storage door, use butt hinges. Space three hinges evenly at the top, center, and bottom of the door. The butt hinges should be mortised.

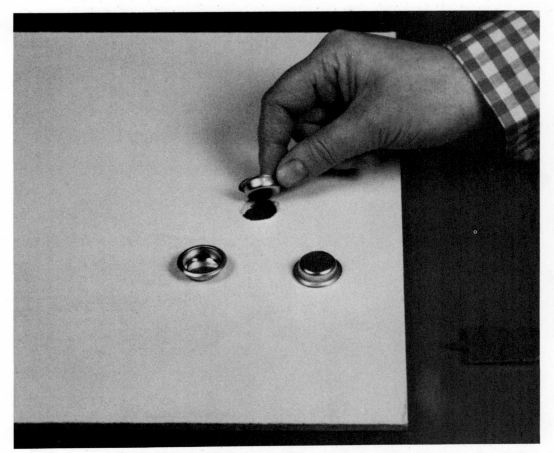

Tempered hardboard makes excellent sliding cabinet doors because the material is dimensionally stable, absolutely flat, and fairly easy to finish with paint and enamel. For finger pulls, you can buy recessed finger-pull hardware. The pulls are simply inserted into a hole you drill in the panel, as shown. A little epoxy will hold the pull in position. If you prefer not to use any hardware, drill the hole, sand the rim smooth, and finish the panel.

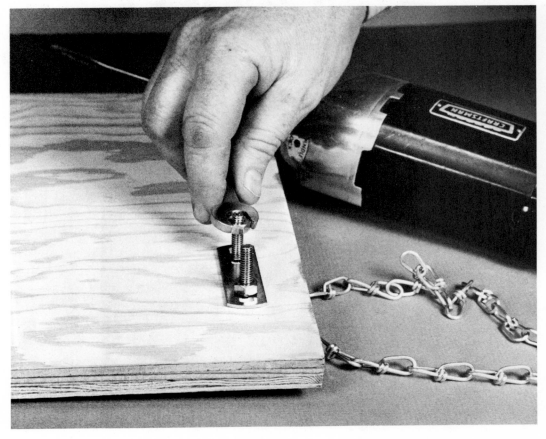

Hanging shelves require hooks in the ceiling (screwed into a joist or rafter) and a U-bolt fastener for the chain. Thread the chain on the U-bolt before you secure the bolt to the shelving. U-bolts are available in a variety of sizes; drill holes in the shelves for the threaded shanks of the bolts, and run the nuts over a flat washer. This helps to distribute the weight load.

Handmade closet pole supports start with a block of 2- by 4-inch lumber. With an expansion bit, drill a hole in the 2 by 4, as shown. Use ¾-inch galvanized pipe for the pole. Mount the pipe with regular pipe flanges, which are screwed to a stud in the wall (on both sides of the pole) or mounted with Molly or toggle bolts. You can buy closet pole hardware, if you don't want to make the handmade supports.

Connect the drilled hole with a crosscut saw or backsaw, and trim the support to the depth you want it to be—at least a couple of inches. Drill pilot holes for the screw fasteners, and mount this support on the wall with screws by attaching to the studs or by using toggle bolts. The closet pole simply nestles in the notch.

Index